By BILLY GRAHAM

THE SECRET OF
HAPPINESS

JESUS' TEACHING ON HAPPINESS

AS EXPRESSED IN THE BEATITUDES

DOUBLEDAY & COMPANY, INC.

Garden City, New York, 1955

TO MOTHER AND FATHER,

WHOSE DEDICATED LIVES

TAUGHT ME THE SECRET OF HAPPINESS.

BOOKS BY BILLY GRAHAM

Peace with God
The Secret of Happiness

PREFACE

I sat down to write a book on "The Greatest Sermon Ever Preached"—the Sermon on the Mount—but I got no further than the eight Beatitudes. The more I read them, meditated on them and studied them, the more I realized that Christ was giving a formula for personal happiness that applied to anyone, no matter what his race, geography, age or circumstance!

When trying to put on paper these thoughts, I decided to consult with other writers. I was amazed to find how little has been written on the Beatitudes. Most Biblical commentaries skip hurriedly over them—yet in these few statements of Jesus is almost the whole depth and scope of His teaching. The Beatitudes are revolutionary! Startling! Deeply profound, and yet amazingly simple! If applied on a universal scale, they could transform the world in which we live. If you apply these simple formulas in your own personal life, you can never be the same!

Ten thousand pages would not be enough to exhaust the meaning of these remarkable statements of the Master; I have only touched the high spots. Although in one sense the Beatitudes are repetitious as Jesus was driving home to His rapt and startled listeners not many points but one point: happiness in this life . . . and eternal life to come!

If by happiness we mean serenity, confidence, contentment, peace, joy and soul-satisfaction, then Jesus was supremely "happy." We never read of His laughing, though I am sure He did. He was not given to pleasure-seeking, hilariousness, jokes or poking fun at others. Nor was His happiness dependent on outward circumstances. He did not have to have an outward stimulus to make Him happy. He had learned a secret

v

that allowed Him to live above the circumstances of life and fear of the future. He moved with calmness, certainty and serenity through the most trying circumstances—even death! What was His secret? He gave it to us in the Beatitudes. Let's go with Christ and discover the secret of happiness!

CONTENTS

THE SECRET OF HAPPINESS

THE SEARCH FOR HAPPINESS

A French philosopher recently said, "The whole world is on a mad quest for security and happiness." The president of Harvard University has said, "The world is searching for a creed to believe and a song to sing."

A Texas millionaire confided, "I thought money could buy happiness—I have been miserably disillusioned." A famous film star broke down. "I have money, beauty, glamour and popularity. I should be the happiest woman in the world, but I am miserable. Why?" One of Britain's top social leaders said, "I have lost all desire to live, yet I have everything to live for. What is the matter?" A man went to see a psychiatrist. He said, "Doctor, I am lonely, despondent, and miserable. Can you help me?" The psychiatrist suggested that he go to the circus and see a famous clown who was said to make even the most despondent laugh with merriment. His patient said, "I am that clown." A college senior said, "I am twenty-three. I have lived through enough experiences to be old, and I am already fed up with life." A famous Grecian dancer of yesteryear once said, "I have never been alone but what my hands trembled, my eyes filled with tears, and my heart ached for a peace and happiness I have never found." One of the world's great statesmen said to me, "I am an old man. Life has lost all meaning. I am ready to take a fateful leap into the unknown. Young man, can you give me a ray of hope?"

Our materialistic world rushes on with its eternal quest for the fountain of happiness! The more knowledge we acquire, the less wisdom we seem to have. The more economic security we gain, the more boredom we generate. The more leisure pleasure we enjoy, the less satisfied and contented we are with life. We are like a restless sea, finding a little peace here and a little pleasure there, but nothing permanent and satisfying. So the search continues! Men will kill, lie, cheat, steal, and war to satisfy their quest for power, pleasure, and wealth, thinking thereby to gain for themselves and their particular group peace, security, contentment, and happiness.

Yet inside us a little voice keeps saying, "We were not meant to be this way—we were meant for better things." We have a mysterious feeling that there is a fountain somewhere that contains the happiness which makes life worth while. We keep saying to ourselves that somewhere, sometime we will stumble onto the secret. Sometimes we feel that we have obtained it—only to find it illusive, leaving us disillusioned, bewildered, and unhappy.

The happiness which brings enduring worth to life is not the superficial happiness that is dependent on circumstances. It is the happiness and contentment that fills the soul even in the midst of the most distressing of circumstances and the most bitter environment. It is the kind of happiness that grins when things go wrong and smiles through the tears. The happiness for which our souls ache is one undisturbed by success or failure, one which will root deeply inside us and give inward relaxation, peace, and contentment, no matter what the surface problems may be. That kind of happiness stands in need of no outward stimulus.

Near my home is a spring that never varies its flow at any season of the year. Floods may rage near by, but it will not increase its flow. A long summer's drought may come, but it will not decrease. It is perennially and always the same. Such is the type of happiness for which we yearn.

Man by nature and instinct is left unsatisfied without at least three things: *First,* because he was created in the image of God, man is a lost and lonely wanderer upon the earth apart from fellowship with his Creator, after whose fashion he was formed. To have a vague knowledge that He exists is not enough. Man must be assured that he is not alone in

2

the world, that a more adequate intelligence and power is guiding his destiny.

Second, man is confused and perplexed apart from truth. He needs the truth as animals do not—not just the truth of the physical sciences and mathematics, but the truth about his being: his beginnings, his purpose, his conflicts, and his future.

Third, man needs peace. Not merely a nondescript, so-called peace of mind—but a peace which frees him from all of life's distracting conflicts and frustrations, a peace of soul which permeates his entire being, a peace that operates through the trials and burdens of life.

Eight times in the Beatitudes—which someone has called the "beautiful attitudes"—Jesus used the word *blessed.* This word *blessed* could have been translated "happy," although it carries a far richer tone than the everyday content of our English word. That is why "blessed" guards well against its reduction and perversion. His first words were: "Happy are ye." And then followed the formula of Jesus for happiness. Certainly if anyone had genuine happiness and blessedness, it was Jesus. He knew its secret, and in these Beatitudes He unveils it to us.

The Beatitudes are not the whole of Jesus's teaching, nor even the Sermon on the Mount. We have just come through a generation in which sincere men made the profound mistake of thinking that Jesus's main role was that of a social reformer, and that he merely came as an examplar of the ideal life. But He was more, much more. He is the Savior, who died for sinners, bearing their transgressions upon the cross. He died to save men who had violated the divine ideal and who were powerless in their unregenerate natures to achieve it.

The best modern scholarship is discovering once again that even the Sermon on the Mount, and the Beatitudes as well, cannot be isolated from the fact of Jesus's saviorhood. The Old Testament had taught that the Christ was to be meek. He was to turn mourning into joy; righteousness was to be His meat and drink; even upon the cross it was His deepest hunger and thirst.

This is another way of saying that, in reality, Jesus Christ is the perfect man of the Beatitudes. He alone, in the history of the human race, experienced fully what He tells us about the happiness and blessedness of life. What He tells us, He tells us as the Savior who has redeemed us and who bids those who sincerely profess our discipleship to follow in His steps.

Christ's message when he was upon the earth was revolutionizing and understandable. His words were simple yet profound. And they shook men. His words provoked either happy acceptance or violent rejection. Men were never the same after listening to Him. They were invariably better or worse. Men either followed Him in love or turned away in anger and indignation. There was a magic in His gospel which prompted men and women to decisive action. He had a "He that is not with me is against me" attitude.

The men who followed Him were unique in their generation. They turned the world upside down because their hearts had been turned right side up. The world has never been the same. History took a sharp turn for the better. Men began to behave like human beings. Dignity, nobility, and honor followed in the wake of Christianity. Art, music, and science, sparked by this new interpretation of life's meaning, began to progress and develop. Man began at long last to resemble again the "image of God" in which he was created. Society began to feel the impact of the Christian influence. Injustice, inhumanity, and intolerance were dislodged by the tidal wave of spiritual power which was released by Christ.

Centuries have rolled by since that initial surge of spiritual life. The stream of Christianity has flowed unceasingly, sometimes at flood tide but more often at ebb tide. Man-made tributaries have flowed into it, polluting and adulterating it. Deism, Pantheism, and, of late, Humanism and blatant Naturalism have flowed like muddy currents into the main stream of Christian thought, so that the world has had difficulty in distinguishing the real from the false.

True Christians were supposed to be happy men! Our generation has become well versed in Christian terminology, but is remiss in the actual practice of Christ's principles and teachings. Hence, our greatest need today is not more Christianity but more true Christians.

The world can argue against Christianity as an institution, but there is no convincing argument against a man who through the spirit of God has been made Christlike. Such a man is a living rebuke to the selfishness, rationalism, and materialism of the day. Too often we have debated with the world on the letter of the law when we should have been living oracles of God, seen and read of all men.

It is time that we retrace our steps to the source and realize afresh the curative qualities of the river of salvation.

Jesus said to the woman at Jacob's well: "Whosoever drinketh of the water that I shall give him shall never thirst." This sin-sick, disillusioned woman was the symbol of the whole race. Her longings were our longings! Her heart-cry was our heart-cry! Her disillusionment was our disillusionment! Her sin was our sin! But her Savior can be our Savior! Her forgiveness can be our forgiveness! Her joy can be our joy!

I invite you to go with me on a thrilling journey, an adventuresome quest! The object of our search? The secret of happiness. The place? Galilee! Let us roll back the pages of time two thousand years.

It's a hot, sultry day with the sweltering wind spinning little dust whirls and carrying them swiftly down the winding road by the Sea of Galilee. There is an air of expectancy in the atmosphere we breathe. The wind skips happily across the surface of the ancient sea. We hear voices raised in an excited, feverish pitch as friend calls a greeting to friend. Along every trail leading from Galilee little groups of people begin to gather. The word has spread abroad that Jesus is returning to Galilee.

Suddenly He and His little band of followers emerge over the brow of a little hill on the Capernaum road, and immediately in their wake is a vast multitude of people from Decapolis, Jerusalem, Judea, and from beyond Jordan.

Quickly the word spreads from mouth to mouth: "Jesus is

coming!" Other multitudes from Tiberias, Bethsaida and Capernaum soon appear and join the others. Together they follow the little band of thirteen robed men. As they reach the summit of the hill where the gentle winds from the plains sweep over them, affording relief from the sun, Jesus stops and motions for them to sit down and rest.

The air is tense. It is a moment to be captured and held for eternity. The crowd hushes as Jesus climbs atop a large red rock and is seated. In the valley on the deserted road, a lone camel rider wends his way along the trail toward Tiberias. A quiet falls upon the multitude as their faces gaze expectantly at Jesus. Then He opens His mouth and begins to speak.

What He said there on that Mount of Beatitudes in faraway Palestine was to go down in history as the most profound, sublime words ever spoken! There in reverent, measured, simple words He revealed the secret of happiness—not a superficial happiness of time and space, but a happiness which would last forever.

His first word was "happy." Immediately His listeners must have pricked up their ears, as we are prone to do. In the pages to follow it is my prayer that you will do even more: prick up your ears . . . open your heart . . . surrender your will. Then you will begin living life with a capital *L*, find a contentment and joy that crowd the futility and vainness out of the daily walk, and discover the secret of happiness!

II

HAPPINESS THROUGH POVERTY

"Blessed are the poor in spirit:
for theirs is the kingdom of heaven."

A French leader has said that if the whole world had enough to eat, money to spend, and security from the cradle to the grave, they would ask for nothing more.

I have often asked myself the question: would that make people happy? And I have answered it just as quickly by saying an emphatic "No!" I know too many rich people who are miserable. There are people with everything that money can buy who are tormented, confused, bewildered, and miserable! Yet how many times I have heard people say, "If only I had a little security, I could be happy." Or, "If only I could have a fine home, new automobiles, and a winter cottage in Florida, I would be content."

However, Jesus made it plain that happiness and contentment are not found this way. He stated that security and riches do not in themselves bring happiness and contentment to the soul.

The Sermon on the Mount was delivered to two distinct groups of people: the *multitude* and the *disciples of Christ.* We can therefore assume that it contains significance and meaning for both the disciples and the multitude, else Jesus would not have addressed it to both.

It gave the *disciples* a glimpse into the lofty spiritual Promised Land in which they were to live as the followers of Christ. It revealed the high ethical plane on which they were to live. It showed that to be a Christian was no mere child's play.

As for the *multitude,* it was an unveiling of what it actually meant to be a follower of Christ. Up to that time Jesus had been to them a fascinating and intriguing miracle worker. His person was magnetic, His manner winsome, His voice compelling. His entire being marked Him as a man of unusual power. He was a master teacher, a formidable debater, a compassionate healer: the gentlest and the sternest of men. Never had they heard anyone like Him.

These people, whose lives were monotonously humdrum in that unromantic faraway land, responded to this Galilean. To spend a day following Him through the villages where He healed the sick, blessed little children, and talked about the kingdom of God was a never to be forgotten experience.

But on this particular day many who followed Him were to be disillusioned. Religion to them had been superstition and meaningless ceremony. It little occurred to them that there was any relevance between religion and life. They had given up ever being happy; and if they ever knew the meaning of the word *happy*, they had forgotten it.

But Jesus was to put the words *blessed* and *happy* back into their vocabularies—and even better, He was to put them into their very hearts and lives.

When Jesus opened his mouth, the first word that fell from his lips was "happy." This word means "blessed, contented, or highly favored." *Happy?* Could any word have been more incongruous? Those who listened that day were far from being blessed or happy. Dupes of the Roman Empire were they, conquered, vanquished, and subdued. Poor, dejected, ill-clad, and pawns of an alien government, their lives were without hope and expectation. Happy? How could their miserly lives be highly favored, blessed, and contented?

Quickly on the heels of that first word followed five others: "Happy are the poor in spirit." If Jesus had omitted the last two words, they would have all rejoiced, for they were all poor. But Jesus said "the poor in spirit."

Wondering, they listened on. Hidden in these seemingly cryptic words was the first foundational secret of happiness. At first it sounds like a contradiction. We usually think of

people who are poor as being unhappy. But Jesus teaches that
happiness is found through poverty.

What kind of poverty did Jesus have in mind? Did He mean
those who had very little of this world's goods? No!

FIRST: If you are to be poor in spirit, *you must be aware
of your spiritual poverty.*

No man is more pathetic than he who is in great need and
is not aware of it. Remember Samson? Standing there in the
valley of Sorek, surrounded by the lords of the Philistines,
". . . he wist not that the Lord was departed from him."[1]

It has been truly said: "No man is so ignorant as he who
knows nothing and knows not that he knows nothing. No man
is so sick as he who has a fatal disease and is not aware of it.
No man is so poor as he who is destitute and yet thinks he
is rich."

The pitiable thing about the Pharisees was not so much their
hypocrisy as it was their utter lack of knowledge of how poor
they actually were in the sight of God. There is always something pathetic about a man who thinks he is rich when he is
actually poor, who thinks he is good when he is actually vile,
who thinks he is educated when he is actually illiterate.

Jesus gave us a dramatic story about a man who had mis-
taken ideas concerning poverty and riches. This man, in a self-
satisfied soliloquy, one night said: "Soul, thou hast much goods
laid up for many years; take thine ease, eat, drink, and be
merry."[2]

It had never occurred to him that the soul cannot subsist
on goods and that the heart cannot be nourished by wine and
food. Because of his stupidity and his attaching an undue importance to material things, God said: "Thou fool."[3] And to
all of those of all ages who are tempted to reason falsely as he
did, God said: "So is he that layeth up treasure for himself,
and is not rich toward God."[4]

[1] Judges 16:20.
[2] Luke 12:19.
[3] Luke 12:20.
[4] Luke 12:21.

You have a body with eyes, ears, nose, hands, and feet. This body has certain legitimate desires and appetites: the appetite for food and drink, the appetite for sex, the appetite for fellowship.

But the Bible teaches that you are more than a body—you are actually a living soul! Your soul was created in the image of God. Just as your body has certain characteristics and appetites, so does your soul. The characteristics of the soul are personality, intelligence, conscience, and memory. Your soul longs for peace, contentment, and happiness.

In the world in which we live, we give most attention to satisfying the appetites of the body and practically none to the soul. Consequently we are one-sided. We become fat physically and materially, while spiritually we are lean, weak, and anemic.

The soul, created in the image of God, cannot be fully satisfied until it knows God aright. Only God can resolve the deepest longings, desires, and appetites of the soul.

You may have the glamour of the movie queen or you may have the riches of a Texas millionaire and still not find happiness, peace, and contentment. Why? Simply because you have given attention to the body but none to the soul.

The soul actually demands as much attention as the body. It demands fellowship and communion with God. It demands worship, quietness, and meditation. Unless the soul is fed and exercised daily, it becomes weak and shriveled. It remains discontented, confused, restless.

Many people turn to alcohol to try to drown the cryings and longings of the soul. Some turn to a new sex experience. Others attempt to quiet the longings of their souls in other ways. But nothing but God ever completely satisfies, because the soul was made for God, and without God it is restless and in secret torment.

The first step to God is a realization of your spiritual poverty. The poor in spirit do not measure the worth of life in earthly possessions, which fade away, but in terms of eternal realities, which endure forever. Wise is the man who openly confesses his lack of spiritual wealth and in humility of heart cries, "God, be merciful unto me, a sinner."

In God's economy, emptying comes before filling, confession before forgiveness, and poverty before riches. Christ said there is a happiness in that acknowledgment of spiritual poverty which lets God come into our souls.

Now, the Bible teaches that our souls have a disease. It is worse than dread cancer, polio, or heart disease. It is the plague that causes all the troubles and difficulties in the world. It causes all the troubles, confusions, and disillusionments in your own life. The name of the disease is an ugly word. We don't like to use it. But it's a word that the psychiatrists are beginning to use once again. In our desire to be modern, we had almost forgotten it, but once again we are beginning to realize that it is the root of all man's troubles. It is *sin*.

Man has sinned against his Creator. God is a holy, righteous, and just person. He cannot allow sin to enter His presence. Consequently, sin has come between God and man.

Now, there must be a confession that we have broken His laws and are willing to renounce our sins, and the acknowledgment that without His fellowship and favor life is empty and doomed. This is not easy! All of us have pride, though it may be expressed in various ways. We do not like to confess that we are wrong or that we have failed. But God says: "All have sinned, and come short of the glory of God."[5] We have failed to live up to the divine standard. We have not only missed His goals for us but also perverted them. We must confess our sin as the first step to happiness, peace, and contentment!

This generation, encouraged by many second-rate philosophies, has tried in vain to live oblivious to God. The current resurgence of religion in the world is a mass confession that humanism has failed. Like the Laodiceans of old, we have said, "I am rich, and increased with goods, and have need of nothing"[6]; but we have discovered that our riches, like our

[5] Romans 3:23.
[6] Revelation 3:17.

beauty, is only skin-deep and is not sufficient to satisfy our eternal souls.

Let us face this fact: We came into the world with nothing, and we will leave it with nothing.

Where do we get the notion that man's idea of success and God's are the same? You have written a book; you are a clever manager and promoter; you are a talented artist; you are independently rich; you have achieved fame and fortune. Without the gifts of intelligence, imagination, personality, and physical energy—which are all endowed by God—where would you be?

Are we not born poor? Do we not die poor? And would we not be poor indeed without God's infinite mercy and love? We came out of nothing; and if we are anything, it is because God is everything. If He were to withhold His power for one brief instant from us, if He were to hold in check the breath of life for one moment, our physical existence would shrivel into nothingness and our souls would be whisked away into an endless eternity.

Those who are poor in spirit recognize their creatureliness and their sinfulness—but more, they are ready to confess their sins and renounce them.

SECOND: If you are to be poor in spirit, *you must receive the riches that Christ has provided by his death and resurrection.*

Recently, medicine has been making rapid advances all over the world. In discovering cures for new diseases, men are finding new vaccines to prevent and cure dreaded diseases.

Would it not be wonderful if man could find an absolute cure for the troubles of human nature? Suppose we could give a shot in the arm to the whole human race that would fill men with love instead of hate, with contentment instead of greed. This would immediately solve all the problems that the world faces at this moment.

Our daily papers record that there is discontentment and unhappiness all over the world as a result of greed, ambition, lust, prejudice, and evil desire. If men could only be content in whatever state they find themselves; if men could love their fellow men regardless of the color of the skin or the shape of the nose; if those who "have" would show compassion on the "have-nots"; if greedy men would give up their unholy ambition for power—would not this world be a different place in which to live?

Suppose, also, a cure could be found for the past mistakes, failures and sins of mankind. Suppose by some miracle all the past could be straightened out, all of life's tangles could be unraveled and the broken strings of life could be repaired. It would seem that such a cure would cause a world-wide stampede!

The most thrilling news in all the world is the fact that there is a cure! A medicine has been provided! Man can be forgiven of all sin! The cobwebs that have collected in his life can be removed!

The sin, confusion, and disillusionment of life can be replaced by righteousness, joy, contentment, and happiness. A peace can be imparted to the soul that is not dependent on outward circumstances. This cure was provided by Jesus Christ two thousand years ago on the cross of Calvary.

On almost every church in the Western world there is a cross. Why? Why has the cross become the symbol of Christianity? It is because on the cross Christ shed his blood, which has become the cure for sinners who will recognize their spiritual poverty and receive Him as their Savior, Master, and Lord.

The death of Christ on that first Good Friday was no mere accident. It was an act of a loving God to reconcile men to himself. Sin had come between man and God. Man could not be happy and contented apart from God. Therefore, in loving grace, God sent his son to bear our sins and to take the penalty and judgment that we deserved.

However, God requires something of *you*. You must confess your spiritual poverty, renounce your sins, and turn by faith to his son, Jesus Christ. When you do that, you become born again. He gives you a new nature. He puts a little bit of heaven down in your soul. Your life changes. Contentment, peace, and happiness come into your soul for the first time.

I have searched the world over in my travels for contented and happy men. I have found such men only where Christ has been personally and decisively received. There is only one permanent way to have peace of soul that wells up in joy, contentment, and happiness, and that is by repentance of sin and personal faith in Jesus Christ as Savior. Has such a moment come to your life? Have you had the experience of receiving Christ? It is not simply an emotional experience. It is a simple surrender of the will to Christ. Do you really want happiness? Then you will have to pay the price of humbling yourself at the foot of the cross and receiving Christ as Savior.

THIRD: If you are to be poor in spirit, *you must be conscious of your dependence on God.*

Jesus said something about becoming like children before we can enter the kingdom of heaven. Children are dependents. That is to say, they depend upon their parents for protection and care. Because of their relationship and position they are not poor; but if it were not for their established relationship with their parents, they could be poor indeed.

As God's children, we are His dependents. The Bible says: "Like as a father pitieth his children, so the Lord pitieth them that fear Him."[7]

Dependent children spend little time worrying about meals, clothing, and shelter. They assume, and they have a right to, that all will be provided by their parents.

Jesus said: "Take no thought, saying, What shall we eat? or What shall we drink? or Wherewithal shall we be clothed? . . . But seek ye first the kingdom of God . . . and all these things shall be added unto you."[8]

Because God is responsible for our welfare, we are told to cast all our care upon Him, for He careth for us. Because we are dependent upon God, Jesus said: "Let not your heart be

[7]Psalm 103:13.
[8]Matthew 6:31, 33.

14

troubled."[9] God says, "I'll do the worrying—don't give it a thought—leave it to me."

Dependent children are not backward about asking for favors. They would not be normal if they did not boldly make their needs known.

God has said to his dependent children: "Therefore come boldly to the throne of grace, that we may obtain mercy, and find grace to help in time of need."[10] God is keenly aware that we are dependent upon Him for life's necessities. It was for that reason that He said: "Ask, and it shall be given you; seek, and ye shall find; knock, and it shall be opened unto you."[11]

Happy is the man who has learned the secret of coming to God daily in prayer. Fifteen minutes alone with God every morning before you start the day can change circumstances and remove mountains!

But all of this happiness and all of these unlimited benefits which flow from the storehouse of heaven are contingent upon our relationship to God. Absolute dependency and absolute yieldedness are the conditions of being His child. Only His children are entitled to receive those things that lend themselves to happiness; and in order to be His child, there must be the surrender of the will to Him.

We must admit we are poor before we can be made rich. We must admit we are destitute before we can become children of adoption.

When we realize that all our own goodness is as filthy rags in God's sight and become aware of the destructive power of our stubborn wills, when we realize our absolute dependence upon the grace of God through faith and nothing more, then we have started on the road to happiness.

Man does not come to know God through works—he comes to know God by faith through grace. You cannot work your way toward happiness and heaven, you cannot moralize your

[9] John 14:1.
[10] Hebrews 4:16.
[11] Matthew 7:7.

15

way, you cannot reform your way, you cannot buy your way. It comes as a gift of God through Christ.

FOURTH: If you are to be poor in spirit, *you must willingly deny yourself that you might better serve Christ.*

The poor in spirit are those who are willing to sell out their stock in themselves and to do as Jesus said: "Deny himself, and take up his cross, and follow me."[12]

Our modern philosophy of self-reliance and self-sufficiency has caused many to believe that man can make the grade without God. "Religion," they argue, "may be all right for certain emotional people, but you can't beat a man who believes in himself."

But alas, this self-confident generation has produced more alcoholics, more dope addicts, more criminals, more wars, more broken homes, more assaults, more embezzlements, more murders, and more suicides than any other generation which ever lived. It is time for all of us, from the intellectuals on down, to take stock of our failures, blunders, and costly mistakes. It is about time that we are putting a little less confidence in ourselves and a little more trust and faith in God.

The rich young ruler who came to Jesus was so filled with his piety, his riches, and his greed that he revolted when Jesus informed him that the price of eternal life was to "sell out" and come and follow Him. He went away sorrowfully, the Bible says, because he could not detach himself from himself. He found it impossible to become "poor in spirit" because he had such a rich estimate of his own importance.

All around us are arrogance, pride, and selfishness: these are the results of sin. From the heavens comes a voice speaking to a tormented, bankrupt world: "I counsel thee to buy of me gold tried in the fire, that thou mayest be rich; and white raiment, that thou mayest be clothed, and that the shame of thy nakedness do not appear; and anoint thine eyes with eyesalve, that thou mayest see . . . Behold, I stand at the door, and knock: if any man hear my voice, and open the door, I will come in to him, and will sup with him, and he with me."[13]

[12] Matthew 16:24.
[13] Revelation 3:18, 20.

Heaven in this life and heaven in the life to come is not on a monetary standard. Nor can flesh and blood find the door to the kingdom of heaven with its contentment, peace, joy, and happiness. Only those who are poor in spirit and are rich toward God shall be accounted worthy to enter there, because they come not in their own merits but in the righteousness of the Redeemer.

"Happy are the poor in spirit: for theirs is the kingdom of heaven."

III

HAPPINESS THROUGH MOURNING

*"Blessed are they that mourn:
for they shall be comforted."*

There comes a time in our lives when good-natured, well-meant cheers like "Buck up, old man" and "Cheer up, old boy" fail to hoist us out of the doldrums. Because our needs are deeper than psychological, such suggestions only seem to make keener our feeling of helplessness.

The truth is: Man, regardless of his cleverness, his achievements and his gadgets, is a spiritual pauper without God.

Christ's message was directed to one specified group—to the "poor," the poor in spirit. Christ said: "The Spirit of the Lord is upon me, because he hath anointed me to preach the gospel to the poor."[1] This does not mean that Christ's message was only for the financially poor, the socially poor, or the intellectually poor. It meant that it was for those cognizant of their spiritual poverty. That was the first Beatitude. It was the dominant note upon which this celestial anthem of truth was composed.

If we would find genuine happiness, we must begin where Jesus began. If we would live beatific lives, we must live by the Beatitudes.

This second Beatitude, "Happy are they that mourn," at first seems paradoxical. Do crying and joy go together? How can one possibly be happy while he is in the throes of mourning? How can one extract the perfume of gladness from the gall of sorrow?

But rest assured that there is deep and hidden significance here, for remember, Jesus was speaking to all men of all

[1] Luke 4:18.

18

beliefs and of all ages and was revealing to them the secret of happiness.

The present age is definitely not an age of mourning. This century could well go down in history not as a century of progress but as "the century of superficiality." The popular exclamation "So what!" aptly describes the attitude of many toward life. Many think that so long as we have sleek automobiles to ride leisurely in, TV and movies to entertain us, luxurious homes to live in, and a million gadgets to serve us that what happens to our souls does not matter. "So what! Laugh, and the world laughs with you; weep, and you weep alone." The apostles of mirth therefore put on their grimacing masks, turn the volume up on their TV or open the accelerator on their convertibles, and plunge into their superficial living.

Now, I am not gunning for TV addicts or hot-rod fiends in particular, but I do strongly contend that life is more than "skin-deep." Look at your popular comedians! Underneath the feigned smirks and the pretended smiles are the furrows and lines of seriousness and sobriety. Although it is their business to make you laugh, they are well aware that life is a solemn business.

Jesus did not mean "Blessed are the morose, the miserable, or the sullen." The Pharisees made a masquerade of religion, rubbed ashes on their faces to appear religious, but He strongly rebuked them for that. "Be not, as the hypocrites, of a sad countenance,"[2] He said.

Who was it that said, "Some people's religion is like a man with a headache—he can't afford to give up his head, but it hurts him to keep it"?

What did He mean when He said: "Happy are they that mourn"? Certainly He did not mean to imply that a special blessing is promised to "crybabies," "sob sisters," or the emotionally upset. This verse was not intended to be a comfort for abnormal psychopathic cases, which have somehow become mentally warped. No, it was addressed to normal, average people for the purpose of showing them how to live happier, fuller, richer lives.

[2] Matthew 6:16.

Let us begin with the word *mourning* itself. It means "to feel deep sorrow, to show great concern, or to deplore some existing wrong." It implies that if we are to live life on the higher plane that we are to be sensitive, sympathetic, tenderhearted, and alert to the needs of others and the world.

There are five kinds of mourning which I believe were implied in this most significant saying of our Lord. The word here employed by Jesus covers such a wide range of attitudes that five shades of meaning are implied. We should prayerfully ponder each one of them.

First: *The mourning of inadequacy.*

Jeremiah, the weeping prophet who mourned not in self-pity but for a wayward, lost world, said: "O Lord, I know that the way of man is not in himself: it is not in man that walketh to direct his steps."[3]

Now, before you can become strong, you must first realize that you are weak. Before you can become wise, you must first realize that you are foolish. Before you can receive power, you must first confess that you are weak. You must lament your sins before you can rejoice in a Savior. Mourning, in God's sequence, always comes before exultation. Blessed are they that mourn their unworthiness, their helplessness, and their inadequacy.

Isaiah, the mighty prophet of God, knew by experience that one must bow the knee in mourning before one can lift the voice in jubilation. When his sin appeared ugly and venomous in the bright light of God's holiness, he said: "Woe is me! for I am undone; because I am a man of unclean lips . . . for mine eyes have seen the King, the Lord of hosts."[4]

No man can be satisfied with his goodness after he has beheld the holiness of God. But our mourning over our unworthiness and sinfulness should be of short duration, for God has said: "I, even I, am He that blotteth out thy transgressions for mine own sake, and will not remember thy sins."[5]

Isaiah had to experience the mourning of inadequacy before

[3] Jeremiah 10:23.
[4] Isaiah 6:5.
[5] Isaiah 43:25.

he could realize the joy of forgiveness. If you have no sense of sorrow for sin, how can you know the need of repentance?

In God's economy, you must go down into the valley of grief before you can scale the heights of spiritual glory. You must become tired and weary of living alone before you seek and find the fellowship of Christ. You must come to the end of "self" before you really begin to live.

The mourning of inadequacy is a weeping that catches the attention of God. The Bible says: "The Lord is nigh unto them that are of a broken heart; and saveth such as be of a contrite spirit."[6]

We have received hundreds of letters from people who tried desperately to "get hold of themselves," who in their own strength tried to shake off their habits, their sins and their nasty dispositions—but all in vain. Finally in desperation they came to Christ, and in him they found strength to be more than conquerors.

Experience reveals that we are inadequate. History proves that man is inadequate. The Bible declares that you are inadequate to save yourself. Christ's coming to the world proves the inadequateness of the race.

The happiest day of my life was when I realized that my own ability, my own goodness, and my own morality was insufficient in the sight of God and I publicly and openly acknowledged my need of Christ. I am not exaggerating when I say that my mourning was turned to joy and my sighing into singing.

Happy are they that mourn for the inadequateness of self, for they shall be comforted with the sufficiency of God.

Another kind of mourning is, second: *The mourning of repentance.*

Following the consciousness that we are inadequate comes the awareness of the reason for our insufficiency—sin. We as individuals have no control over the fact of sin in the universe, but as creatures of choice we are responsible for its presence in our lives. Because "all have sinned, and come short of the

[6] Psalm 34:18.

21

glory of God,"[7] all need to mourn the fact of sin in their lives.

One technique of modern psychoanalysis is the association of present conflicts with past experiences. Sometimes when patients of psychiatry confess to past sins, they experience a certain release from their feelings of guilt. But since psychiatry is a science of the mind, it can do nothing for the heart. Only Christ is the Physician of the soul.

God has said: "Turn ye even to me with all your heart . . . with weeping, and with mourning."[8]

The mourning of repentance is not the weeping of self-pity, not regret over material losses nor remorse that your sins have been found out. It is a change of direction, an alteration of attitudes, and a yielding of the will. It is your small part in the plan of salvation. But even so, the act of repentance does not merit or earn your worthiness to be saved—it only conditions your heart for the grace of God.

The Bible says: "Repent ye therefore, and be converted, that your sins may be blotted out, when the times of refreshing shall come from the presence of the Lord."[9] Your part is repenting. God will do the converting, the transforming, and the forgiving.

It will not be easy to bend your warped, stubborn will; but once you do, it will be as though a misplaced vertebra has snapped back into place. Instead of the stress and tension of a life out of harmony with God will come the serene peace of reconciliation. Your nerves will sense that your mind and heart are relaxed, and they will send this happy news over their network to every fiber of your body: "Old things are passed away; behold, all things are become new."[10]

Just as pain precedes birth, mourning over sin comes before spiritual rebirth. I do not mean to imply that in your experience there will be loud, violent weeping over the sin in your life—your sorrow for sin may come quietly, with little or no emotion. But there will be a sincere sorrow for the evils of your

[7] Romans 3:23.
[8] Joel 2:12.
[9] Acts 3:19.
[10] II Corinthians 5:17.

life and a disposition to turn to God for help and salvation. The Bible says: "For godly sorrow worketh repentance."[11]

There is yet another aspect of this Beatitude, "Happy are they that mourn." There is, third: *The mourning of love.*

In many of the older cars the fuel gauge used to contain a red liquid, and its level in the gauge corresponded to the level of fuel in the tank. As the liquid was in the gauge, so it was in the tank.

If you would know the measure of your love for God, just observe your love for your fellow men. Our compassion for others is an accurate gauge of our devotion to God.

The Bible puts it this way: "Let us love one another: for love is of God; and every one that loveth is born of God, and knoweth God. . . . And this commandment have we from Him, That he who loveth God love his brother also."[12]

Some time ago, with some friends, I went through a museum in San Francisco. Among other things, we saw a collection of instruments of torture which were employed by religious people to force other people to believe as they did. History is largely the record of man's inhumanity to man.

This age in which we live could hardly be described as conducive to a sensitiveness of the needs of others. We have developed a veneer of sophistication and hardness. This generation, it seems, would rather see a prize fight than fight for a prize. Not only has the song "Rescue the Perishing, Care for the Dying" disappeared from our song books, but its theme has disappeared from our hearts.

Abraham Lincoln once said, characteristically: "I am sorry for the man who can't feel the whip when it is laid on the other man's back."

Much of the world is calloused and indifferent toward mankind's poverty and distress. This is due largely to the fact that for many people there has never been a rebirth. The love of God has never been shed abroad in their hearts.

Many people speak of the social gospel as though it were separate and apart from the redemptive gospel. The truth is:

[11] II Corinthians 7:10.

[12] I John 4:7, 21.

23

There is only one gospel. We must be redeemed, we must be made right with God before we can become sensitive to the needs of others. Divine love, like a reflected sunbeam, shines down before it radiates out. Unless our hearts are conditioned by the Holy Spirit to receive and reflect the warmth of God's compassion, we cannot love our fellow men as we ought.

Jesus wept tears of compassion at the grave side of a friend. We mourned over Jerusalem because as a city it had lost its appreciation of the things of the spirit. His great heart was sensitive to the needs of others.

To emphasize the importance of man's love for man, He revised an old commandment to make it read: "Thou shalt love the Lord thy God with all thy heart . . . and thy neighbor as thyself."[13]

St. Francis of Assisi had discovered the secret of happiness when he prayed:

> *Lord, grant that I may seek rather*
> *To comfort than to be comforted,*
> *To understand than to be understood,*
> *To love than to be loved;*
> *For it is by giving that one receives,*
> *It is by self-forgetting that one finds,*
> *It is by forgiving that one is forgiven,*
> *It is by dying that one awakens to eternal life.*

This generation is rough and tough. I heard a little boy boasting one day about how tough he was. He said, "On the street I live on, the farther out you go the tougher they get, and I live in the last house."

Tears shed for self are tears of weakness, but tears of love shed for others are a sign of strength. You are not as sensitive as you ought to be until you are able to "weep o'er the erring one and lift up the fallen." And until you have learned the value of compassionately sharing others' sorrow, distress, and misfortune, you cannot know real happiness.

Another kind of mourning which brings comfort is, fourth: *The mourning of soul travail.*

[13] Luke 10:27.

This may seem cryptic, but it represents a very real and a very profitable kind of mourning. The Bible says: "As soon as Zion travailed, she brought forth her children."[14] This refers to the continual flow of prayer which rises out of the Christian heart for a world unborn spiritually.

God worked in a miraculous way in London in the early part of 1954, and 38,000 men and women made their decisions for Christ. Their coming was not the result of one man's work or the efforts of a group of men—it was the product of much prayer by many people around the world. God has said: "If my people . . . pray . . . then will I hear from heaven."[15]

Before three thousand people were brought into the Church on the day of Pentecost, the disciples had spent ten days in prayer, fasting, and spiritual travail.

John Knox, with an all-consuming soul-concern for his country, prayed: "Give me Scotland, or I die!" His earnest travail was rewarded with a spiritual rebirth in his land. This is what is termed "praying in the Spirit." It is the manifestation of a deep spiritual concern for others, and it is instilled by the Spirit of God.

The Bible says: "For we know not what we should pray for as we ought: but the Spirit Himself maketh intercession for us with groanings which cannot be uttered."[16]

This kind of prayer can leap over oceans, speed across burning deserts, spring over mountains, and bound through jungles and carry the healing, helping power of the gospel to the objects of our prayer.

This kind of mourning, this quality of concern, is produced by the presence of God's spirit in our lives. That "the Spirit Himself maketh intercession" indicates that it is actually God pleading, praying and mourning through us. Thus we become colaborers with God, actual partners with Him: our lives are lifted from the low plane of selfishness to the high plane of creativeness with God.

John Knox travailed, and the Church in Scotland broke into

14 Isaiah 66:8.
15 II Chronicles 7:14.
16 Romans 8:26.

new life. John Wesley travailed in prayer, and the Methodist movement was born. Martin Luther travailed, and the Reformation was under way.

God desires that Christians be concerned and burdened for a lost world. If we pray this kind of prayer, an era of peace may come to the world and hordes of wickedness may be turned back. "As soon as Zion travailed, she brought forth her children."[17]

The last kind of mourning we shall deal with is, fifth: *The mourning of bereavement.*

Nowhere has God promised anyone, even His children, immunity from sorrow, suffering, and pain. This world is a "vale of tears," and disappointment and heartache are as inevitable as clouds and shadows. Suffering is often the crucible in which our faith is tested. Those who successfully come through the "furnace of affliction" are the ones who emerge "like gold tried in the fire."

The Bible teaches unmistakably that we can triumph over bereavement. The Psalmist said: "Weeping may endure for a night, but joy cometh in the morning."[18]

Self-pity can bring no enduring comfort. The fact is, it will only add to your misery. And unremitting grief will give you little consolation in itself, for grief begets grief. Ceaseless grieving will only magnify your sorrow. Don't peddle your sorrows and bewail your bad fortune—that will only depress others. Sorrow, or mourning, when it is borne in a Christian way, contains a built-in comfort. "Happy are they that mourn: for they shall be comforted."

There is comfort in mourning because we know that Christ is with us. He has said: "Lo, I am with you alway, even unto the end of the world."[19] Suffering is endurable if we do not have to bear it alone; and the more compassionate the Presence, the less acute the pain.

How often when a child have you stubbed your toe, bruised a leg, or cut a hand, and, running to the arms of your mother,

17 Isaiah 66:8.
18 Psalm 30:5.
19 Matthew 28:20.

you there sobbed out your woe? Lovingly caressing you and tenderly kissing the hurt, she imparted the magic of healing; and you went your way half healed and wholly comforted. Love and compassion contain a stronger balm than all the salves and ointments made by man.

Jesus said, "Let not your heart be troubled . . . believe . . . in me."[20] When faith is strong, troubles become trifles.

There is also comfort in mourning because in the midst of mourning God gives a song. God says in Job 30:9: "I am their song." His presence in our lives changes our mourning into song, and that song is a song of comfort.

This kind of comfort is the kind which enabled a devout Englishman to look at a deep, dark hole in the ground where his home stood before the bombing and say, "I always did want a basement, I did. Now I can jolly well build another house like I always wanted."

This kind of comfort is the kind which enabled a young minister's wife in a church near us to teach her Sunday school class of girls on the very day of her husband's funeral. Her mourning was not the kind which had no hope—it was a mourning of faith in the goodness and wisdom of God; it believed that our Heavenly Father makes no mistakes.

Before the power of the atom was discovered, science had to devise a way to "smash" the atom. The secret of the atom's immeasurable and limitless power was in its being crushed.

So, in our lives, there is a blessedness in mourning. The sensitive soul sings the sweetest. The bullfrog's croak is not to be compared with the canary's song, because the frog is less sensitive to pain, cold winds, and privation. The higher the form of life, the greater is the ability to suffer.

Dr. Edward Judson, in speaking of the life of his father, Adoniram Judson, at the dedication of the Judson Memorial Church in New York City, said, "Suffering and success go together. If you are succeeding without suffering, it is because others before you have suffered; if you are suffering without succeeding, it is that others after you may succeed."

"Happy are they that mourn." They are happy because they

[20] John 14:1.

know that their pain, their distress, and their privation are the travail of a new creation, the birth pangs of a better world. They are happy because they are aware that the Master Artist —God—is employing both light and shadow to produce a masterpiece worthy of divine artistry.

They are also made to glory in their infirmities, to smile through their tears, and to sing in the midst of their sorrow because they realize that in God's economy "if we suffer, we shall also reign with him."[21]

[21] II Timothy 2:12.

IV

HAPPINESS THROUGH MEEKNESS

"Blessed are the meek:
for they shall inherit the earth."

Most of us seek short cuts to happiness. We search for the gold nuggets of spiritual satisfaction on the surface instead of in the depths, where they are found in abundance. It is only natural to follow the line of least resistance, forgetting all the while that heat and light are both products of resistance, a resistance which releases the latent forces of life.

Many of us are like the man out West who had a junk yard. He labored hard and long, buying and selling the old salvage he gathered from the back alleys of the city. But one day he discovered that his junk yard was located on an oil field. He hired a drilling crew, and soon the black gold flowed abundantly from the bosom of the earth. His junk yard was transformed into a veritable mine of wealth which knew no limits.

In these Beatitudes we have a mine of spiritual gold. To many it seems too good to be true, so they go their way, scratching around on the surface of life, picking up salvage in the form of gadgets, gold, and gimmicks. Because they ignore the challenge and the promise of these secrets of happiness, they miss the key to radiant living and remain spiritual paupers, writhing in a misery of their own making.

They forget that what happens *within* them is more important than what happens *to* them. Because they have built no inner fortifications, they fall a prey to the Enemy. They become filled with resentments and are baffled by frustration and depressed by disillusionment.

Do you think that God would have bothered to send His

Son to the world if man had been able to face life and eternity alone? Christ's coming to the world proved that God was not happy with man's unhappiness. He sent Him not only that we might have eternal life but that we might have life here and now, and that we might have it more abundantly—Life with a capital *L!*

Jesus's teaching was unique and different. He took religion out of the theoretical category and placed it in the practical. He used no qualifying statements or phrases in declaring His way of life. He didn't use such phrases as "I venture to say" or "Perhaps it's this way" or "It is my considered opinion."

He spoke with authority! He spoke with finality! He spoke as though He knew . . . and He did!

His was not the soft, empty conjecture of the philosopher who professes to search for truth but readily admits he has never found it. It was more the confident voice of the mathematician who gives his answers unhesitatingly because the proof of the answer can be found within the problem.

In this third Beatitude we have the words "Happy are the meek: for they shall inherit the earth." Has it ever occurred to you that there is happiness in meekness? The dictionary says that the word *meek* means "mild, submissive, and compliant." The truth of the matter is: most of us know very few people who are mild, submissive, and compliant.

Could it be that Christ wanted his followers to be like a subdued puppy which comes crawling into his master's presence whipped and beaten? Is happiness the result of forced submission? Certainly not!

Jesus is not trying to convey the thought that God is an autocrat whose ego can be satisfied only by coerced yielding. Nothing could be further from the truth. There is no happiness in being compelled to do what you do not wish to do. No slaves are more miserable than those who constantly resent their servitude. It would be against God's nature, as well as against man's free moral agency, to ask an allegiance which is not freely offered.

God conducts himself in keeping with His righteousness.

He will never violate our freedom to choose between eternal life and spiritual death, good and evil, right and wrong. His ultimate goal is not only to glorify Himself but also to make happy relationship with His crowning creation—man. Never will He make any demands which encroach upon man's freedom to choose.

Or does the meekness to which Jesus refers mean weakness? Does it mean that a special blessing is to be given to the feeble, the frail, or the fragile? Surely not! The disciples were meek, but not weak. They were disciplined, but not subdued.

Or does Jesus refer to those who are by nature mild-tempered? Some people are born with nicer dispositions than others. Their mild manner is not so much the product of prayer and spiritual grace as it is a thing of heredity. They are mild because their mother or their father or their grandmother was mild-mannered. This is an admirable trait, but Jesus surely didn't refer to these fortunate few who by nature have good dispositions. That would mean that many who have dispositions like buzz saws could never know this happiness to which He refers.

Jesus, in his characteristic way, was saying something quite shocking and quite revolutionary to His listeners in these words: "Happy are the meek." He was saying something quite the opposite to our modern concept of the way to happiness.

We say, "Happy are the clever, for they shall inherit the admiration of their friends"; "Happy are the aggressive, for they shall inherit prosperity"; "Happy are the talented, for they shall inherit a career"; "Happy are the rich, for they shall inherit a world of friends and a house full of modern gadgets."

Jesus did not say, "Be meek, and you shall inherit the earth." He, more than anyone else, knew that meekness was a gift of God, a result of a rebirth.

Moses was meek, but he was not meek by nature. He slew an Egyptian in anger, and on more than one occasion he showed that his meekness was not merely a natural attribute. When he found the children of Israel turning from the Lord and worshiping idols, he waxed indignant and dashed to the ground the tables of stone upon which were inscribed the Ten Commandments. His meekness quite obviously was contrary to his nature. It was a miracle of God!

Peter was not meek by nature. He waxed angry and cut off the ear of a guard who had come to take Jesus. He swore profusely and angrily when accused of being one of Jesus's disciples. And yet he became one of the meekest of men and one of the strongest, most virile exponents of Christianity. Where did he get his meekness?

Paul, before his conversion, was not meek. Proudly and brutally he apprehended all Christians and sought to destroy them. He was bigoted, selfish, and vaunted. But when he wrote his warm and affectionate letter to the churches of Galatia, he said, among other things: "The fruit of the Spirit is . . . gentleness, goodness . . . meekness."[1] His meekness was something God-given, not something man-made.

It is not our nature to be meek. On the contrary, it is our nature to be proud and haughty. That is why the new birth is so essential to each of us. That is why Jesus very frankly and pointedly said not only to Nicodemus but to everyone of us: "Ye must be born again."[2]

Meekness begins there! You must have a change of nature. Do you want this happiness? Then you must be born again— this is the first step! If you are too proud, stubborn, and willful to take this first step, then you do not qualify to inherit the earth.

When we reject this command of Christ, we automatically forfeit our right to His subsequent promises. We cannot end right when we start wrong. If there is no rebirth, there can be no imparted meekness. And if there is no meekness, there can be no genuine happiness.

Arrogance has its own built-in misery. The arrogant person may offend others, but he hurts himself more.

I was once stung by a honeybee. The sting hurt me, but it hurt the bee more—the bee died as a result of that thrust, but I didn't.

[1] Galatians 5:22, 23.
[2] John 3:7.

Jesus was not issuing a command in this Beatitude nor saying, "You ought to be meek, that is the way to live." No! He was saying that if we want to find the secret of happiness, that if we want to enjoy living, then "meekness" is a basic key.

Meekness is a gem of many surfaces. It is a spiritual attribute with many aspects. Let us hold this jewel of spiritual beauty up to the light of truth as we behold its many-faceted loveliness.

FIRST: *Meekness means gentleness.*

The word *gentle* was rarely heard of before the Christian era, and the word *gentleman* was not known. This high quality of character was a direct by-product of Christian faith.

The world in the last few years has reverted to a sort of barbarism. As practical Christianity declined, rudeness and savagery increased. But all this toughness—this ruthlessness which has found expression in a series of tough, bloody wars— has left its mark on the individual member of society.

Our children are given toys representing violence: guns, tanks, fighting planes, and soldiers. Our entertainment media have catered to our savagery by giving us films of intrigue, murder, war, and lawlessness. Our pulp magazines have added fuel to the flame by dramatizing the hatreds, the lusts, and the passions of human nature. Of course our comic books have contributed to our moral chaos by exploiting our children and making them violence-minded.

This reversion to barbarism now affects whole areas of our social life. Neighbors quarrel with neighbors. Fighting is a major problem in our schools, and the "gang wars" of the teen-agers have come to present a serious menace in our cities. Fathers and mothers wrangle and bicker. Homes are disintegrating. High government officials in Washington engage in name-calling and in heated disputes not at all in keeping with the dignity of their office.

Why and how has all this savagery crept into our social life? It is because we have forgotten Jesus's words: "Happy are the meek: for they shall inherit the earth."

We have glamorized vice and minimized virtue. We have played down gentleness, manners, and morals; while we have played up rudeness, savagery, and vice. We have reverted to the barbaric era of "tooth and claw," "the survival of the fittest," and the philosophy of "might is right." We are rich in knowledge but poor in wisdom; rich in the know-how of war but sadly lacking in gentleness, meekness, and faith. Individually, we are mechanisms of resentment, irritation, bitterness, and frustration!

The Bible says: "The wisdom that is from above is first pure, then peaceable, *gentle,* and easy to be entreated, full of mercy and good fruits, without partiality, and without hypocrisy."[3]

I have seen tough, rough, hardened men open their hearts by faith, receive Christ as Savior and become gentle, patient, merciful gentlemen.

I remember, when we were in London, the Ford Motor Company loaned us two new Fords and employed two drivers to take our team to their various assignments. One of the chauffeurs was a typical rough-and-tough worldly fellow, who had missed very little of what the world had to offer. He came to the meetings and looked on the scene perfunctorily with an occupational detachment. But one night he was moved to go to the counseling room and make his decision for Christ. You never saw such a change come over a man! His hardness disappeared; his veneer of sophistication melted away. He was a new creature! He threw away his racy literature, began to memorize the New Testament, and took on the true marks of a Christian gentleman. The fruit of the Spirit is ". . . gentleness, goodness . . . meekness."[4]

SECOND: *Meekness involves yieldedness.*

The word *yield* has two meanings. The first is negative and the second is positive. It means "to relinquish, to abandon"; and also "to give." This is in line with Jesus's words: "He that loseth (or abandoneth) his life . . . shall find it."[5]

We have heard the modern expression "Don't fight it—it's bigger than both of us." Those who are meek do not fight back at life. They learn the secret of surrender, of yielding to God. He then fights for us!

[3] James 3:17.
[4] Galatians 5:22, 23.
[5] Matthew 10:39.

The Bible says: "For as ye have yielded your members servants to uncleanness and to iniquity . . . even so now yield your members servants to righteousness unto holiness."[6]

Instead of filling your mind with resentments, abusing your body by sinful diversion, and damaging your soul by willfulness, humbly give all over to God. Your conflicts will disappear and your inner tensions will vanish into thin air.

Then your life will begin to count for something. It will begin to yield, to produce, to bear fruit. You will have the feeling of belonging to life. Boredom will melt away, and you will become vibrant with hope and expectation. Because you are meekly yielded, you will begin to "inherit the earth" of good things which God holds in store for all who trust Him with their all.

Even science teaches in unmistakable terms the Christian concept of entire surrender. Thomas Huxley once wrote Charles Kingsley: "Science says to sit down before the facts as a little child, be prepared to give up every preconceived notion, be willing to be led to whatever end Nature will lead you, or you will know nothing."

Happy are the meek. Happy are the yielded. Happy are those who trustingly put their lives, their fortunes, and their future in the capable hands of their Creator. Happy are those who "let go and let God."

THIRD: *Meekness implies tameness.*

A broken horse contributes much more to life than a wild donkey. Energy out of control is dangerous; energy under control is powerful.

God does not discipline us to subdue us, but to condition us for a life of usefulness and blessedness. In His wisdom He knows that an uncontrolled life is an unhappy life, so He puts reins upon our wayward souls that they may be directed into the "paths of righteousness." That is what God seeks to do with us: to tame us, to bring us under proper control.

He does in the spiritual realm what science does in the physical realm. Science takes a Niagara River with its violent turbulence and transforms it into electrical energy to illuminate

6 Romans 6:19.

a million homes and to turn the productive wheels of industry.

God took Peter—a zealot, a political reactionary of his day—and diverted his energy and his unbounding enthusiasm to high purposes instead of low, and he helped lead a movement which reshaped the world.

He took Matthew—a suave, tricky politician, who knew the political ropes well enough to keep from dangling from one of them by the neck—and, putting the bridle of grace upon him, changed him into an agent of blessing.

God had to do a job of taming with each of the disciples. Taming was not a matter of doing away with their powers and their energies but of redirecting them.

You have a *temper!* There is nothing unique about that. Most people have tempers, in varying degrees of course. God does not ask that you get rid of that temper. But He does say that if you are to be happy, it must be brought under control and rechanneled to proper use. God cannot use a man without a temper as well as one with a controlled temper. There are too many professed Christians who never get "wrought up" about anything; they never get indignant with injustice, with corruption in high places, or with the godless traffics which barter away the souls and bodies of men.

You have an *ego*—a consciousness of being an individual! Of course you do. But that doesn't mean that you are to worship yourself, to think constantly of yourself, and to live entirely for self. Common sense tells you that your life would be miserable if you followed that course. God is infinitely more concerned about your happiness than you could possibly be. He says, "Deny yourself, and follow me."

There is many a person in the insane asylum today who thought excessively about himself, to the exclusion of God and others. Hypochondriacs who have a fanciful anxiety about their health will never be well regardless of their physical condition.

You have a *tongue* and a *voice*. These instruments of speech can be used destructively or employed constructively. You can use your tongue to slander, to gripe, to scold, to nag, and to quarrel; or you can bring it under the control of God's Spirit and make it an instrument of blessing and praise.

The twentieth-century version of James 3:3 says, "When we put bits into the horses' mouths to make them obey us, we control the rest of their bodies also." Just so, when we submit to the claims of Christ upon our lives, our untamed natures are brought under His control. We become meek, tamed, and "fit for the Master's service."

FOURTH: *Meekness connotes forbearance.*

That is a word which has been almost dropped from our modern vocabulary. It means to abstain from condemning others, to refrain from judging the actions and motives of those about you.

The Bible says: "With all lowliness and meekness, with long-suffering, forbearing one another in love."[7]

This generation is quick with the deadly thrust but slow with the ointment of healing. The harsh criticism of others and unfair appraisals of those about you may hurt them, but it hurts *you* more. The unjust condemnation of others has a boomerang effect. You hurl your vindicative indictments with the hope of crippling others, but, alas, you discover that you are hurt more than they are.

Many a person is lonely today because he has driven away by his own bitterness the very friends he needed. Many a wife has discovered that scolding and nagging will never win a husband but often ends in divorce.

Meekness and forbearance are "musts" if you are to live harmoniously in society and if you want to build a happy family life.

The Bible says: "Speak evil of no man ... but gentle, showing all meekness unto all men."[8] You cannot be happy as long as you magnify the faults of others and minimize their virtues. This is a good way to frighten away your friends, forfeit your domestic happiness, and fritter away a rosy future.

Here is the Christian answer to neighborhood quarrels, to family fusses and community feuds: "Forbearing one another,

[7] Ephesians 4:2.
[8] Titus 3:2.

and forgiving one another, if any man have a quarrel against any: even as Christ forgave you, so also do ye."[9]

There is a story told of a devout old deacon who, goaded apparently beyond endurance by the persistent malice of an enemy, publicly avowed to "kill him." His enemy heard of his intentions and awaited sardonically to see what the harmless old saint would do. Actually, instead of rendering evil for evil, the old deacon sought out every opportunity to do his enemy good. This was at first a source of merriment and some slight annoyance, but when at last the deacon rendered an unquestioned sacrificial service to his enemy by risking his life to save his wife from drowning, the deadlock between them was broken.

"All right," said his enemy, "you've done what you said you would do. You've killed me—or at least you've killed the man I *was.* Now, what can I do for you?"

This world is not yet impervious to a solid Christian act! What the world needs is not more Christianity but more Christians who practice Christian forbearance and forgiveness.

And, last: *Meekness suggests patience.*

This is a high-strung, neurotic, impatient age. We hurry when there is no reason to hurry, just to be hurrying. This fast-paced age has produced more problems and less morality than previous generations, and it has given all of us a set of jangled nerves.

Impatience has produced a new crop of broken homes, a million or more new ulcers, and has set the stage for more world wars. In no area of our lives has it been more damaging than on the domestic scene. This homely little couplet bespeaks the rack and ruin it has wrought in our homes:

> *Theirs was a "beef stew" marriage,*
> *And their case was somewhat crude—*
> *The wife was always "beefing,"*
> *And the husband, always "stewed."*

But the Bible says: "But let patience have her perfect work, that ye may be perfect and entire, wanting nothing."[10]

I know of a woman—a professed Christian—who, though

[9] Colossians 3:13.
[10] James 1:4.

38

good in many respects, was very impatient. Her pastor one day spoke to her husband about his soul, and the man replied, "My wife is a good homemaker, but if religion would make me as impatient as she is, I want no part of it."

The minister had a frank talk with the woman, and in tears and humility she confessed that her sin was the sin of impatience. A few days later her husband came in from fishing. As he walked through the living room with rod in hand, he accidentally knocked over a prized vase that went shattering to the floor. His wife ran into the room, and he braced himself for the second crash—a tirade of words from his nervous wife. But instead, she smilingly said, "Think nothing of it, dear, accidents happen in the best of families."

We will not pursue the story any further except to say that a few weeks later he made his decision for Christ and became a staunch worker in the church.

The world believes that Christianity is a good thing, but Christians have too often failed to "adorn the doctrine" by not living meek and patient lives.

"Happy are the meek: for they shall inherit the earth." Only those who are contrite, humble, and submissively dependent upon God can inherit the earth of radiance, joy, and contentment.

Jesus said to Saul: "It is hard for thee to kick against the pricks."[11] The pricks he referred to were goads which were in the harness of the oxen to keep them under control. They were not put there to harm the ox but to make him useful, to direct his energies toward constructive channels.

Many of you have been "kicking against the pricks." Your quarrel has not been so much with others, as you thought, as it has been with yourself. God does not want you to live in constant rebellion against life, its seeming injustices, its hurts and its wrongs. He bids you to stop your futile strivings, to surrender your resentments, to yield your will, and to exercise gentleness and patience. Then you will be happy, and others about you will see Christ in you and will be drawn toward Him.

Meekness is not something you can acquire by yourself. It is

[11] Acts 9:5; 26:14.

not something you can get in college or in a scientific laboratory. It is not something you inherit. It is God-given! Jesus said: "Take my yoke upon you, and learn of me; for I am meek and lowly in heart: and ye shall find rest unto your souls."[12]

Go into an electric-appliance dealer's store and notice all of the pretty colored light bulbs in the showcase. You can almost hear them say, "I know I'm a light bulb, but why can't I shine with the radiance of that one up there in the fixture?" The reason *is* that it is not connected with the source of power.

God is no respecter of persons. You deserve your just share of happiness. You have the same capacity for God as anyone else. Don't stand back lamenting your bad luck and your bad breaks in life. Take Christ's yoke upon you, "and ye shall find rest unto your soul"!

"But I can't live it! I would surely fail in the attempt to be a Christian!"

Jesus said: "Take my yoke upon you." It is His yoke, and you may rest assured that He will bear the heavy part of the load.

Before he left his disciples, Christ promised that he would send a Comforter to help them in the trials, cares and temptations of life. This word *comforter* means "one that helps alongside." He is the Holy Spirit, the powerful Third Person of the Trinity. The moment you are born again He takes up residence in your heart.

You may not emotionally feel Him there, but here again you must exercise faith. Believe it! Accept it as a fact of faith! He is in your heart to help you to be meek!

We are told that He sheds the love of God abroad in our hearts. He produces the fruit of the Spirit: "love, joy, peace, long-suffering, gentleness, goodness, faith, meekness, temperance."[13] We cannot possibly manufacture this fruit in our own cannery. It is supernaturally manufactured by the Holy Spirit who lives in our hearts!

Yield to Him . . . surrender to Him . . . give Him control of your life. Then through the meekness you receive from Him you will find happiness!

[12]Matthew 11:29.
[13]Galatians 5:22, 23.

40

V

HAPPINESS THROUGH HUNGER AND THIRST

"Blessed are they which do hunger and
thirst after righteousness:
for they shall be filled."

"Two verbs have built two empires," wrote St. Augustine, "the verb *to have* and the verb *to be*. The first is an empire of things, material possessions and power. The second is an empire of the Spirit, things that last."

This fourth Beatitude of Christ expresses a crucial, central truth. When Jesus spoke these words: "Happy are they which do hunger and thirst after righteousness," He addressed them to the multitude.

The multitude on that torrid, sultry day in Palestine symbolizes the great parade of men and women down through the centuries. What He said to them, He says to us and has been saying to all men through the years. Most of the people in that throng were disfranchised spiritually, socially, and economically. Their hungers were very deep, but none of their needs were more deep-seated than their spiritual longings and yearnings.

You can give man social and economic freedom, but if his thirst for fellowship with God remains unquenched, he will still behave like an animal. Witness the prosperity of Western civilization at this very moment. We have everything a machine age can provide, yet boredom and unhappiness have reached an all-time high and our morals have plunged to an all-time low. The reason: our hunger for God has not been satisfied.

A man and wife visited an orphanage where they hoped to adopt a child. In an interview with the boy they wanted, they told him in glowing terms about the many things they could give him. To their amazement, the little fellow said, "If you

41

have nothing to offer except a good home, clothes, toys, and the other things that most kids have—why—I would just as soon stay here."

"What on earth could you want besides those things?" the woman asked.

"I just want someone to love me," replied the little boy.

There you have it! Even a little boy knows that "man shall not live by bread alone."[1]

The heart cannot be satisfied with gadgets, knickknacks, and juke boxes. We were created "just a little lower than the angels"[2] and our souls can never subsist on the husks of this pleasure-seeking world. Our deeper yearnings and longings can be met only by a renewed fellowship with the One in whose image we were created: God.

"Happy are they which do hunger and thirst after righteousness: for they shall be filled."

We can all understand the metaphor which Jesus employed here—hunger. We have all experienced sometime in our lives the gnawing pain, the dizziness, and the faint feeling which accompanies intense hunger. We know what it is to experience the dry parchedness of thirst. So, quite naturally, we come to attention when He says: "Happy are they which do hunger and thirst."

But what happiness is there in hunger and thirst?

Well, to begin with, hunger is a sign of life. Dead men need no food, they crave no water.

The Bible teaches that it is possible through lack of spiritual earnestness to harden your heart as Pharaoh did long ago. This is one of the most dangerous processes that can take place in the human soul. It is possible through sin to harden your heart against God so long that you lose all desire for God. Then the Scripture says: "God gave them up."[3]

If you have the slightest bit of hunger in your heart for God and righteousness, then it is a certain sign that it is not too

[1] Matthew 4:4; Luke 4:4.

[2] Hebrews 2:7.

[3] Psalm 81:12; Romans 1:24.

hardened to be receptive to the voice and message of Christ. You are yet alive and sensitive to the Spirit's voice.

Those who have no cravings for God, no longings for Christ, and no thirst for the things of the Spirit are not only dead in trespasses and sins, but they are also insensitive to the Spirit's promptings. They are like dead men and are in danger of remaining in a state of spiritual stupor that will lead eventually to eternal death.

A man once told me that he nearly froze to death in the far north. His hands lost their feeling, his feet became numb, and he was overcome with an impulse to lie down in the snow and go to sleep when it dawned upon him that he was freezing to death. He jumped up and ran vigorously until his circulation was stimulated. If he had not suddenly become conscious that he was dying and acted upon that consciousness, he would have frozen to death.

Happy are those who respond to the Spirit's warnings. They alone have hope of being filled.

A hungry man is a normal man. Those who are sick and abnormally upset refuse nourishment, but the normal person craves food. In that sense there is a blessedness in hunger. It is a natural reaction.

The normal person also possesses a spiritual hunger. David said: "As the hart panteth after the water brooks, so panteth my soul after thee, O God."[4]

Isaiah said: "With my soul have I desired thee in the night; yea, with my spirit within me will I seek thee early: for when thy judgments are in the earth, the inhabitants of the earth will learn righteousness."[5]

You were created in the image and likeness of God. You were made for God's fellowship, and your heart can never be satisfied without His communion. Just as iron is attracted to a magnet, the soul in its state of hunger is drawn to God. Though you, like thousands of others, may feel in the state of sin that the world is more alluring and more to your liking, someday—

[4] Psalm 42:1.

[5] Isaiah 26:9.

perhaps even now as you read these words—you will ackowl-edge that there is something deep down inside you which cannot be satisfied by the alloy of earth.

Then with David, the Psalmist who had sampled the deli-cacies of sin and had found them unsatisfying, you will say: "O God, Thou art my God; early will I seek thee: my soul thirsteth for thee, my flesh longeth for thee in a dry and thirsty land, where no water is."[6]

The trouble with most of us is that we make happiness our goal instead of aiming at something higher, loftier, and nobler. Unhappiness is like pain—it is only an effect of an underlying cause. Pain cannot be relieved until the cause is removed. Pain and disease go together: disease is the cause, and pain is the effect.

Unhappiness is an effect, and sin is the cause. Sin and unhappiness go together. All was blissful happiness in the Garden of Eden until sin crept in. Then happiness crept out. The two just cannot exist together.

What is this righteousness we are to desire? Is this righteous-ness to which Jesus referred in the fourth Beatitude a religious experience? Is it some mysterious ecstasy which comes to only a few people fraught with cataclysmic emotions and spiritual sensations?

The kind of religious experience which does not produce righteousness in the life is hardly worth seeking. I would be the last to minimize the importance of a definite experience of religion. But religious demonstrations that do not create in us better morals and a Christlikeness of character serve no useful purpose and could certainly do more harm than good. God is holy, and the whole scheme of redemption has holiness for its goal.

Nor is this righteousness to which Jesus referred a perfunc-tory, mechanical performance of religious rites. Jesus taught the futility of holding to religious theory apart from Christian practice when He said: "Except your righteousness shall exceed

[6] Psalm 63:1.

the righteousness of the scribes and Pharisees, ye shall in no case enter into the kingdom of heaven."[7]

Neither is it an abstract, speculative morality so prevalent in the world today. Many people condemn sin in high places but fail to recognize it in their own personal lives. They condemn it in the government and society but condone it in their own hearts.

It is just as sinful in God's sight for an individual to break the marriage vow as it is for a nation to break a treaty.

What is this righteousness that Jesus exhorts us to hunger for? The Bible teaches that God is a holy, righteous, and pure God. He cannot tolerate sin in His presence. However, man has chosen to disregard the divine laws and standards. As a result of man's transgressions, he is called a "sinner." Sin immediately breaks his fellowship with God. Man becomes unrighteous, impure, and unholy in the sight of God. A holy God cannot have fellowship with that which is unholy, unrighteous, and unethical. Therefore, sin breaks off friendship with God. Man is called in the Bible an "alien," an "enemy" to God, and a "sinner" against Him. The only way that man can again have fellowship with God and find the happiness that he longs for is to find some way to possess a righteousness and holiness that will commend him to God.

Many have tried to reform in order to gain favor with God. Some have mutilated their bodies and tortured themselves, thinking thereby to gain favor with God. Others have thought that if they would work hard and live moral lives, they could somehow justify themselves.

But the Bible teaches that all our righteousness—falling short of the divine standard as it does—as is filthy rags in the sight of God. There is absolutely no possibility of our manufacturing a righteousness, holiness, or goodness that will satisfy God. Even the best of us is impure to God.

I remember one day when my wife was doing the washing. The clothes looked white and clean in the house, but when she hung them on the line they actually appeared soiled and dirty in contrast to the fresh-fallen snow.

[7] Matthew 5:20.

45

Our own lives may seem at times to be morally good and decent; but, in comparison to the holiness and the purity of God, we are defiled and filthy.

In spite of our sins and moral uncleanness, God loves us. He decided to provide a righteousness for us. That is the reason that He gave His Son, Jesus Christ, to die on the cross.

Have you ever stopped to think why it is the cross has become the symbol of Christianity? It is because at the cross Jesus purchased our redemption and provided a righteousness which we could not ourselves earn. "The gift of God is eternal life through Jesus Christ our Lord."[8] God has provided on the ground of faith in the atoning death and resurrection of His Son an imputed righteousness for all who will receive it.

This means that God forgives all past sin and failure. He wipes the slate clean. He takes our sins and buries them in the depths of the sea and removes them as far as the east is from the west.

The Omniscient God has the unique ability that man does not have: He has the ability to forget. The God of grace forgets our sins and wipes them completely from His memory forever! He places us in His sight as though we had never committed one sin.

In theological language, this is called *justification*. The Bible says: "Therefore being justified by faith, we have peace with God through our Lord Jesus Christ."[9]

There is no possibility of true happiness until we have established friendship and fellowship with God. And there is no possibility of establishing this fellowship apart from the cross of His Son, Jesus Christ. God says, "I will forgive you, but I will forgive you only at the foot of the cross." He say, "I will fellowship with you, but I will fellowship with you only at the cross." That is the reason it is necessary for us to come to the cross in repentance of our sin and by faith in His Son to find forgiveness and salvation.

Righteousness is something which we do not possess as a natural gift, but it is a God-given gift to be specially received.

[8] Romans 6:23.
[9] Romans 5:1.

46

It is a bit of heaven brought to earth. The righteousness of the God-man is imputed to us in justification, and in sanctification that righteousness is progressively implanted in the believer's heart. It is God's sharing his nature with us. We become partakers of divine life.

Now, God says that only those who hunger after it will receive it. God thrusts this heavenly manna on no one. You must desire it, above everything else. Your yearning for God must supersede all other desires. It must be like a gnawing hunger and a burning thirst.

There are several things that can spoil your appetite for the righteousness of God.

FIRST: *Sinful pleasure* can ruin your appetite for the things of God.

Paul had a young colaborer in the gospel by the name of Demas. Because his appetite for the pleasures of the world was greater than his thirst for God, we hear very little of young Demas. Paul wrote his entire history in nine words: "Demas hath forsaken me, having loved this present world."[10]

Many of us have no appetite for spiritual things because we are absorbed in the sinful pleasures of this world. We have been eating too many of the devil's delicacies.

I once heard the story of a man walking down the road. Behind him followed a pig. A friend called to him and asked him how he got the pig to follow him. He said, "It's very simple. Every step I take, I drop a bean, and the pig likes beans."

Satan goes along the road of life dropping his beans, and we are following him to eternal destruction.

SECOND: *Self-sufficiency* can impair your hunger after God.

No man is so empty as he who thinks he is full. No man is so ill as he who has a fatal disease and yet thinks he is in perfect health. No man is so poor as he who thinks he is rich but is actually bankrupt.

The Bible says: "Because thou sayest, I am rich, and increased with goods, and have need of nothing; and knowest not

10 II Timothy 4:10.

47

that thou art wretched, and miserable, and poor, and blind, and naked."[11]

He that is filled with himself has no room for God in his life. Self-sufficiency can ruin your appetite for the things of Christ.

THIRD: *Secret sin* can take away your appetite for the righteousness of God.

That secret sin you committed has cost a price. You always thought you had got away with it, but the remorse of it still remains in your heart. Those evil resentments you harbor in your breast against your neighbor! The failure to forgive those who have wronged you! When the heart is filled with wickedness, there is no room for God. The jealousies, the envies, the prejudices, and the malices will take away your appetite for the things of the Spirit.

When your life is filled with the husks of prejudice and the chaff of resentment, you can have no thirst for righteousness. If you allow your heart to be filled with Satan's rations, you will have no desire for heaven's manna.

FOURTH: *Neglect of your spiritual life* can take away your appetite for the righteousness of God.

All Christians believe in God, but many Christians have little time for God. They are too busy with everyday affairs to be taken up with Bible reading, prayer, and being thoughtful to their fellow men. Many of them have lost the spirit of a zealous discipleship.

If you ask them if they are Christians, they would probably answer, "I think so," or "I hope so." They may go to church at Easter and Christmas and other special occasions, but otherwise they have little time for God. They have crowded God out of their lives.

The Bible warns against neglect of your soul. It is possible to harden your heart and shrivel your soul until you lose your appetite for the things of God.

This hunger, then, that you should have is a desire to be always right with God. It is a consciousness that all searching for peace of heart except in Him is in vain. It is an admission of

[11] Revelation 3:17.

48

your own futility, your own helplessness to help yourself, and a complete abandonment of yourself to His will.

Like Peter, who stepped out upon the waves of self-sufficiency only to find that they would not bear him up, we cry, "Master, save me, or I perish!"

Like the prodigal son, who sampled the devil's delicacies in the far-off city, we discover that the world's husks fill but do not satisfy. It is then in the knowledge of our real need that we say, "Father, I have sinned against heaven, and before thee. . . . Make me as one of thy hired servants."[12]

The prodigal son's "come-back" began down in the swine pen when he said, "How many hired servants of my father's have bread enough and to spare, and I perish with hunger!"[13] The very moment that he began to hunger, God began to "set the table" for spiritual reunion. His deepest yearnings and longings were not for food but for being reconciled to his father.

Neither is our goal to be blessings, experiences, or even answers to our prayers, taken by themselves. These are all the accompaniment of being right with our Heavenly Father.

God, like the prodigal's father, says to all of those who hunger and thirst after righteousness, "Son, all that I have is thine."

But the key to spiritual satisfaction is being right with God. When we through faith are in the position of sonship, then God's riches become our riches; God's abundance, our abundance; God's power, our power. When a proper relationship has been restored between us and God, then happiness, contentment, and peace of mind will be a natural outgrowth of that restored relationship.

You ask, "How can I start? What do I have to do?"

Jesus said: "You must be converted." The word *conversion* means to "turn around," to "change your mind," to "turn back," and to "return." It is the human act by which man expresses his desire to change the course of his life, to turn toward God, and to live in accordance with divine law. This involves a confession of your sin to God, a renouncing of your sins, a turning from your sins—and then by faith receiving Christ. If it is

12 Luke 15:18, 19.

13 Luke 15:17.

genuine, it has a divine side: regeneration, or the gift of spiritual life by the Holy Spirit.

But many people immediately argue, "I do believe in Christ. I believe in the Church, and I believe in the Bible. Isn't that enough?"

No! You must *receive* Christ.

I may go to the airport. I have a reservation. I have a ticket in my pocket. The plane is on the ramp. It is a big, powerful plane. I am certain that it will take me to my destination. They call the flight three times. I neglect to get on board. They close the door. The plan taxis down the runway and takes off. I am not on the plane. Why? I "believed" in the plane, but I neglected to get on board.

That's just it! You believe in God, Christ, the Bible, and the Church—but you have neglected to actually receive Him in your heart. Your belief has been an impersonal, speculative thing, and you have not entrusted yourself to Him.

The moment you receive Him, the Bible says, you are born again. God's nature enters into your own soul, and you become a son of God in full spiritual fellowship.

This is what we might call the "vertical relationship," the perpendicular affinity between God and man. It is absolutely the first step toward happiness. There is no use reading the rest of this book until you are absolutely sure that you have repented of sin, received Christ by faith, and been born again. The vertical relationship must always precede the "horizontal."

Our sustenance, our supply, our power come from above. Man is like a tram or a streetcar. He must be connected vertically (above) before he can move horizontally. Our relationship must be right with God before it can be right with man. And if this be true, then the converse is equally true—if we are wrong with God, we are wrong with man also.

There is a law in musical tone which says, "Two instruments tuned to the same pitch are in tune with each other." A similar rule in mathematics is: "Two quantities equal to the same quantity are equal to each other."

So two people in tune with God are in tune with each other. Two people in love with Christ have love for each other.

There is another aspect of this righteousness that we are to hunger for. It is the righteousness of a victorious existence in this present life.

The moment you receive Christ as your Lord and Savior, Christ through the Holy Spirit comes to live in your heart. The Scripture says: "Christ in you, the hope of glory."[14] You may not see Him with your natural eye and you may not feel Him with your emotions, but He is there nevertheless. You are to accept Him by faith!

This aspect of righteousness for which we are to hunger is called, in theological language, *sanctification*. Don't let this word frighten you. It actually means "separated" or "clean." In one sense, sanctification is instantaneous. The moment you receive Christ as Savior, the Holy Spirit comes into your heart.

There is also a sense in which sanctification is progressive. You grow in the grace and knowledge of Jesus Christ. Being a Christian is more than just an instantaneous conversion—it is a daily process whereby you grow to be more and more like Christ. When you start out, you start out as a baby. You must be fed on the simple things of the Bible, and you learn to walk in your Christian life gradually. At first you will fall down and make many mistakes, but you are to continue growing.

However, there are many people who have stopped growing. They remain spiritual babes all their lives. I am afraid that this experience is all too common today. Perhaps it is yours.

Do you remember the day when you gave your heart and your life to Christ? You were sure of victory. How easy it seemed to be more than conqueror through Christ, who loved you. Under the leadership of a Captain who had never been foiled in battle, how could you dream of defeat?

And yet to many of you, how different has been your real experience! Your victories have been few and fleeting and your defeats many and disastrous. You have not lived as you feel children of God ought to live.

As Mrs. Hannah Whitehall-Smith reminds us, "You have had, perhaps, a clear understanding of doctrinal truths, but you have not come into possession of their light and power. In your life

14 Colossians 1:27.

51

Christ is believed in, talked about, and served, but He is not filling you hour by hour. You found Christ as your Savior from the penalty of sin, but you have not found Him as your all-sufficient Savior from its power. The joy and thrill of Christian experience is gone."

There is only a dying ember of what used to be a mighty prairie fire for Christ in your soul. In the very depths of your heart you know that your experience is not the scriptural experience. Down through the years it seems that all you can expect from your Christianity is a life of ultimate failure and defeat—one hour failure, and the next hour repenting and beginning again, only to fail again.

We read in the Scriptures that the early church was filled with the Holy Ghost. They had no churches, no Bibles, no automobiles, no planes, no trains, no television, no radio. Yet they turned their world "upside down" for Christ. They instituted a spiritual revolution that shook the very foundations of the Roman Empire. They were young, vigorous, virile, powerful. They lived their lives daily for Christ. They suffered persecution and even death gladly for their faith in Christ.

The reason Communism is making such inroads in the world today is that somewhere along the line the people who were supposed to live Christian lives failed. We have failed to meet the standards and requirements that Jesus set forth. We must not only outpropagandize and outfight Communism, we must outlive it.

The great masses of the unbelieving world are confused as they gaze upon the strife within and between religious bodies. Instead of a dynamic, growing, powerful, Christ-centered Church, we see division, strife, pettiness, greed, jealousy, and spiritual laziness, while the world is standing on the brink of disaster.

The great need in Christendom today is for Christians to learn the secret of daily victory over sin. Thousands of Christians have struggles within themselves.

Paul himself spoke of this struggle. He spoke of desiring to please God, but in himself he found no strength to do so. The things he did not want to do he sometimes did; and the things he wanted to do he did not do. Nearly driven to distraction, Paul shouts out: "Who shall deliver me from the body of this death?"[15]

And in the next verse he records the answer to that all-important, searching, bewildering question when he says: "I thank God through Jesus Christ our Lord."[16]

Christ can be your Deliverer!

Many of you ask the questions: "Why do I, as a Christian, do some of the things I do? Why do I, as a Christian, leave undone the things I ought to have done?"

Many of you name the Name of Christ, but you are living in constant defeat. You have unclean hands, unclean lips, unclean tongues, unclean feet, unclean thoughts, unclean hearts —and yet you claim to be a Christian. You claim Christ, you attend church, you try to pray—and yet you know that there are things in your soul that are not right. You do not have complete and constant victory that is promised in the Scripture. There is no radiance in your face. The spring in your step is gone. The fire in your soul has been quenched.

Yet as you look around, you do know some people who are living different lives. It is stamped on their faces. You can tell it in the way they walk and in the way they talk. They bear the fruit of the Spirit. But you get only snatches of victory. Once in a while you will have a day that seems to be a victorious day over temptation, but then you slide right back into the same old rut of living, and you long and hunger for the righteousness of daily growth.

There are other Christians who have never really learned the Biblical truth of separation: separation from unclean thoughts and unclean habits.

There are some Christians who have learned little of a daily devotional life.

Some time ago a policeman asked me what the secret of victorious living was. I told him that there is no magic formula that can be pronounced. If any word could describe it, I would say *surrender*. The second word I would say would be *devotion*.

[15] Romans 7:24.
[16] Romans 7:25.

Nothing can take the place of a daily devotional life with Christ. Your quiet time, your prayer time, the time you spend in the Word is absolutely essential for a happy Christian life. You cannot possibly be a happy, dynamic, and powerful Christian apart from a daily walk with Christ.

It is unfortunate that even among Christians our conversation is of comparatively small matters. We can quote the batting average of our favorite baseball star, but we are unable to quote a Bible verse other than John 3:16. We are full of talk about our homes, our cars, our television; but we are woefully ignorant of the things of God.

If a sick and dying man should stumble upon our door, we would be incapable of guiding him through his problems to Christ the Savior.

Our spiritual intellects have become poverty-stricken; hence the trite verbal intercourse that passes between us. Our daily conversation when we meet each other, whether it be in the office or on the campus or in the shop, should be concerning the things of God. We should be exchanging spiritual blessings and thoughts that we have received from our daily Bible reading.

It is not enough for us to have been confirmed, or to have made a decision for Christ at an altar, and to hope to walk in the glow of that experience successfully for the rest of our lives. Being human, we have to return and renew our vows and covenants with God. We have to take inventory and spiritual checkups.

Christ is calling Christians today to cleansing, to dedication, to consecration, and to full surrender. It will make the difference between success and failure in your spiritual life. It will make the difference between being helped and helping others. It will make a difference in your habits, in your prayer life, in your Bible reading, in your giving, in your testimony, and in your church membership. This is the Christian's hour of decision!

But many of you ask, "How can I begin?" I would like to suggest that you take all of the sins that you are guilty of and make a list of them. Then confess them, and check them off, remembering that Jesus Christ forgives. The Bible says: "If we confess our sins, He is faithful and just to forgive us our sins, and to cleanse us from all unrighteousness."[17]

Then, after you have confessed every known sin in your life, yield every area of your life. Yield your girl friend, your boy friend, your family, your business, your career, your ambitions, your soul, the innermost thoughts and depths of your heart; yield them all to Christ. Hold nothing back.

Take your eyes and your ears and your hands and your feet and your thoughts and your heart: give them completely and unreservedly to Christ. Then by faith believe that God has accepted your surrender.

Paul said: "I am crucified with Christ: nevertheless I live; yet not I, but Christ liveth in me."[18]

We can reckon ourselves indeed dead unto sin. The Bible says we can be more than conquerors through Him that loved us.

It has been my privilege to know what it means to walk in the way of Christ. What a thrilling, joyous experience it is to wake up every morning and know His presence in the room! What a thrilling, joyous experience it is to know in the evening, when the sun is setting, the peace of God as you go to bed and to sleep, and to sleep the sleep of only those who know Christ! What a joy it is to walk in the eternal and permanent experience of Christ!

Do you hunger for such a walk? Do you long for such joy, peace, contentment, abandonment, and adventure in your own soul? Do you long to produce the fruit of the Spirit, which is "love, joy, peace, long-suffering, gentleness, goodness, faith, meekness, temperance"?[19]

You can have this kind of life now—at this moment—if you are willing to pay the price of complete and absolute surrender! The moment you surrender, Christ, through the Holy Spirit, fills your heart and life. Then you can truthfully say, "I am filled with the Spirit."

First, remember that the Christian life is lived by "Christ in

[17] I John 1:9.
[18] Galatians 2:20.
[19] Galatians 5:22, 23.

you." However, if Christ does not have *all* of you, it is impossible for you to live a happy Christian experience. When He has all of you, then He fills you to overflowing and He produces in you the fruit of the Spirit. It is absolutely impossible for any person to manufacture, generate, or produce the Christian life apart from the power of the Holy Spirit. He stands at this moment ready to enter your heart with a floodtide of blessing if you will surrender every area of your personality and life to Him. It is your birthright! Claim it—believe it—accept it! It's yours *now*.

If this is your hunger and desire, then God will do exactly what He has promised to do: He will fill you. "Happy are they that hunger and thirst after righteousness: for they shall be filled." Every promise God has ever made He has kept. He will fill you now if you are hungry enough to surrender.

Second, God will fill you with His righteousness, because man has no holy longings, no holy cravings that cannot ultimately be satisfied.

We shall not be perfect in thought, word, and deed until we are glorified in the world to come, but the breath of that glory, and a godlikeness of character, is the Christian's proper heritage in this earthly walk. We are *Christians*, and the world should sense to its conviction that, wherever we walk in its midst, a heavenly virtue still goes out from whatever truly bears His Name.

Man hungers for food, and God sends the sun and rain upon the golden fields of grain. The grain is made into flour and flour into bread, and man's physical hunger is satisfied.

Man hungers for love; and God ignites the fire of affection in another heart, and two hearts are made complete in the bonds of holy matrimony.

Man hungers for knowledge, and God raises up institutions of learning, calls men to be instructors, puts it into the hearts of the rich to endow them; and men are satisfied in their thirst for knowledge.

Man hungers for fellowship, and God allows him to build cities where men can share their industry, their knowledge, and their skills.

Don't tell me that God can supply man with an abundance of everything material and yet will let him starve spiritually!

The Bible says: "Hearken diligently unto me, and eat ye that which is good, and let your soul delight itself in fatness."[20]

Again the Bible says: "For the bread of God is He which cometh down from heaven, and giveth life unto the world."[21]

Third, God will satisfy the hunger and thirst of those who desire His righteousness, because He loves the world with an undying affection. He moved heaven and earth to redeem us. Would it seem logical that a father would pay a huge ransom to redeem a son and then forsake him in his hour of hunger? The fact that the initial cost of our salvation was so great leads us to believe that God certainly does not desire that we shall want for anything. A parent who loves his child will not see him starve.

The Bible says: "But my God shall supply all your need according to His riches in glory by Christ Jesus."[22]

This promise "Happy are they which do hunger and thirst after righteousness" is one which makes man responsible to God, and God responsible to man. Our small human part is to hunger and to thirst.

If we have no desire for righteousness, it means only that we have permitted sin and neglect to spoil our desire for fellowship with God. No matter how alluring, attractive, and pleasant the tidbits of the world may seem, they can never satisfy our deeper longings and heart cravings.

We can only know peace of heart and tranquility of mind when we admit and confess our deeper hungers, when we yield completely to God and when we are willing to turn from the synthetic substitutes of the world and drink in the "water of life."

[20] Isaiah 55:2.

[21] John 6:33.

[22] Philippians 4:19.

VI

HAPPINESS THROUGH SHOWING MERCY

"Blessed are the merciful:
for they shall obtain mercy."

Someone asked an old deacon if he were a Christian, and he answered more truly than he realized when he said: "In spots."

Many of us are Christians in certain areas of our lives. We accept the general ideas and ideals of Christianity as being proper and desirable. We go to church on occasion because it seems the right thing to do. We believe in a certain respectability that men ought to be honest, fairly moral, and loyal citizens. But when the question "Are you a Christian?" is put to us bluntly, we are at a loss for an affirmative, positive answer. Inwardly we are ready to confess that if the disciples of Christ had no stronger faith than ours that it is doubtful if Christianity would have been the revolutionary force that it has been in the world.

The simple truth is: for some reason we have failed to take Christ seriously. We have failed somewhere in our consecration and dedication. If we had lived during the day of Crucifixion, we probably would have been with Peter in his denial. Many of us would have been with Judas in his betrayal. Others of us would have taken sides with the crowd rather than with Christ!

In this Beatitude, Jesus puts his finger on the fluttering pulse of modern Christianity. In a few terse words He—the Great Physician—diagnoses a sick and faltering Christianity. In short, He describes one of our troubles as self-centeredness.

Have you ever noticed the personal possessive pronouns used in our everyday conversation: *my* house, *my* problems, *my* trouble, *my* feelings, *my* nerves, *my* family, *my* church, *my* denomination?

Do you remember the rich young ruler who wanted to follow Jesus, but who, when he was told to sell all and give to the poor, went away sorrowful, for he had great possessions?

Jesus knew that one of the real tests of our yieldedness to God is our willingness to share with others. If we have no mercy toward others, that is one proof that we have never experienced God's mercy.

To paraphrase this Beatitude we might say, "They which have obtained mercy from God are so happy that they are merciful to others." Our attitude toward our fellow men is a more accurate gauge of our religion than all of our religious rantings.

Emerson must have been reading the gauge of human mercy when he said: "What you are speaks so loud that I cannot hear what you say."

Jesus summed up the whole matter of genuine Christianity when He said: "If any man thirst, let him come unto me, and drink. He that believeth on me, as the Scripture hath said, out of his inmost soul flow rivers of living water."[1]

Christianity is, first, a coming to Christ—an inflowing of the Living Water; second, it is a reaching for Christ—an outflowing. It is to be shared in love, mercy, and compassion with others.

A body of water which has an inlet but no outlet becomes a stagnant, insect-infested pond. When we think of Christianity as *my* experience, *my* emotions, *my* ecstasy, *my* joy, *my* faith—with no desire to share mercifully with others—we can only boast of stagnation. Not living, vital, flowing Christianity!

Listen to what the Scripture says: "Defend the poor and fatherless: do justice to the afflicted and needy."[2] "Whoso stoppeth his ears at the cry of the poor, he also shall cry himself, but shall not be heard."[3]

Jesus said: "Give to him that asketh thee, and from him

[1] John 7:37, 38.

[2] Psalm 82:3.

[3] Proverbs 21:13.

that would borrow of thee turn not thou away."[4] And: "Give, and it shall be given unto you; good measure, pressed down, and shaken together, and running over, shall men give into your bosom."[5]

In this Beatitude, which we could well term the "outflowing" Beatitude, Jesus is emphasizing the fact that we are to be unchoked channels through which His love and mercy flow to men.

If you have a religion which does not work effectively in everyday life, one which fails to condition your attitudes toward your fellow men and one which makes you a spiritual introvert, you may be sure that you do not know the Christ who spoke these Beatitudes!

Satan does not care how much you theorize about Christianity or how much you profess to know Christ. What he opposes vigorously is the way you live Christ—the way you become an instrument of mercy, compassion, and love through which He manifests Himself to the world. If Satan can take the heart, motive, and mercy out of Christianity, he has killed its effectiveness. If he can succeed in getting us to talk a good case of religion but to live a poor one, he has shorn us of our power.

If we embrace a spiritual, aesthetic gospel only and disregard our obligation to our fellow men, we annul it all. The gospel of the New Testament can come into full blossom only when the seed of the Spirit is buried in the rich soil of human mercy.

It is first an intaking, and then an outgiving. Jesus said in our outgiving we would find happiness.

Some time ago a lady wrote and said, "I am sixty-five years old. My children are all married, my husband is dead, and I am one of the loneliest people in all the world." It was suggested to her that she find a way of sharing her religious faith and her material goods with those around her. She wrote a few weeks later and said, "I am the happiest woman in town.

[4] Matthew 5:42.

[5] Luke 6:38.

I have found a new joy and happiness in sharing with others."

That's exactly what Jesus promised!

What are some of the areas in today's world toward which we can show mercy?

FIRST: We can show mercy by *caring for the social needs* of our fellow men.

When you go to bed tonight, remember that over half of the world's population is hungry, poor, and wretched. Most of these are illiterate people who are unable to read or write. Most of them use farming methods a thousand years old. Many of them are little better than slaves to the big landlords who own the land. They need food, education, clothes, homes, medical care, and—most of all—love. We have a responsibility to these downtrodden peoples of the world.

Did not Jesus feed the multitudes as well as preach the gospel to them? Did He not point out to us the folly of talking religion and failing to put it into action? Did He not say: "Woe unto you, scribes and Pharisees, hypocrites! for ye shut up the kingdom of heaven against men . . . for ye devour widows' houses, and for a pretence make long prayer: therefore ye shall receive the greater damnation"?[6]

Here is one place we have failed! We have theorized about religion and have debated doctrinal matters while the world has been dying in misery without the necessities of life and, in many cases, without hope.

What a selfish, ingrown, wanton people we have become! Little wonder that there is so much boredom, frustration, and unhappiness. The words of Jesus "Happy are the merciful" were certainly apropos for this merciless generation.

Dr. Frank Laubach wrote me recently saying, "In my opinion, the United States must make an all-out effort to help the destitute half of the world out of its misery, or we shall find that the world has gone Communist because of our neglect."

Perhaps you cannot go to these faraway lands, but you can give to missionary and charitable causes that will help build

[6] Matthew 23:13, 14.

61

hospitals, educational institutions, and orphanages and provide the necessities of life to many of these destitute millions.

But let's come closer home. If you only looked, you would find people near you who are in physical need. One Christmas Eve a friend came to my house and said, "Would you like to go out with me distributing Christmas packages up in the mountains?" I was glad to go. And I was in for one of the greatest surprises of my life! I thought everybody in our community had all the necessities of life. But I was taken back into some little mountain valleys where people did not have enough to wear, enough to eat, and could not even afford soap to wash their bodies. Appalled and humbled, I asked God to forgive me for neglecting the people in my own community. I had not even bothered to look around me to see what people's needs were.

If you will ask God to show you, you will find people in your own community who need physical help.

There are others in your community who need a friend. There are many lonely people who never know the handclasp of a friend. They never receive a letter. They sit in their loneliness. Having an interested friend willing to write to them and to visit with them would change their entire lives.

There are others who are lonely and miserable because they perhaps do not have personalities that lend themselves to mixing with other people. I have a friend who went to a social gathering. A harelipped lad with pimples on his face sat over in the corner. No one paid any attention to him. He looked lonely, despondent, and miserable, and completely out of place. My friend went over and spent the evening with him. When he left, he was full of smiles. This friend had shown mercy.

There are a thousand little ways that you can be merciful in your daily lives. There is a hospital near you which you can visit. There are scores of people on hospital beds who long for someone to call on them, to bring them flowers and a cheery smile. You can show mercy by visiting the sick.

SECOND: We can show mercy by *doing away with our prejudices.*

All over the world a new nationalism is rising. Color bars are being broken down while other social barriers are being raised. Prejudice stalks many countries.

The word *prejudice* means "prejudging" or "making an estimate of others without knowing the facts." Prejudice is a mark of weakness, not of strength; it is a tool of the bigot, but never a device of the true Christian. It is one of our great problems in this complex age. It has become an increasing problem insomuch as modern man has forsaken the pathway of Christian mercy and understanding and has chosen to walk the road of intolerance and intrigue.

Emerson referred to the prevailing gentility of yesteryear when he said:

> *He drew a circle that shut me out,*
> *Heretic, rebel, a thing to flout;*
> *But love and me had the wit to win,*
> *We drew a circle that took him in.*

Prejudice is measured by computing the distance between our own biased opinions and the real truth. If we would all be perfectly honest before God, there would be no prejudice. But since most of us by nature are possessed of biased minds and perverted hearts, prejudice is widespread in the world.

Edward R. Murrow once said, "There is no such thing as an objective reporter. We are all slaves of our environment."

All of us have our biases and our prejudices. Despite our improved educational system, our prejudices have grown in the past few years—so we can conclude that education is not the cure for all prejudice.

Even the great Charles Lamb once said: "I am, in plainer words, a bundle of prejudices, made up of likings and dislikings."

Prejudice is a form of robbery, for it robs its victim of a fair trial in the court of reason. It is also a murderer, because it kills the opportunity of advancement for those who are its prey.

Jesus struck at the very core of it when He said: "And why beholdest thou the mote that is in thy brother's eye, but con-

⁷ Matthew 7:3.

63

siderest not the beam that is in thine own eye?"[7] And then He laid down a specific rule against it when He said: "Judge not, that ye be not judged."[8]

The greatest social evil in the world today is prejudice which is oftentimes based upon our own ignorance. I seriously doubt if we would be prejudiced against anyone if we had all the facts in hand. We are quick to judge and prone to denounce that which we do not understand or know or experience.

But how can we be rid of this murderous prejudice?

Only one way: by the process of spiritual rebirth. Prejudice, intolerance, and bigotry must yield to justice, humility, and mercy. This can only happen when there is an infusion of divine power. All of the nuclear scientists in the world— though they have learned to smash the atom!—cannot smash prejudice. All of the world's educators cannot extricate the "root of bitterness" from the human soul. This is an operation which only God can perform.

Listen to the words of Saul of Tarsus, once one of the world's most prejudiced men: "Love suffereth long, and is kind; love envieth not; love vaunteth not itself, is not puffed up. . . . Rejoiceth not in iniquity, but rejoiceth in the truth; Beareth all things, believeth all things, hopeth all things, endureth all things."[9]

What the logic of Greece could not do for Saul, the grace of God did. What the culture of Rome could not do, the grace of God did perform. After his experiences on the Damascus road, the old prejudice melted away. *Mercy* became the key word of his preaching, the theme of his epistles, and the pattern for his conduct. "I beseech you therefore, by the mercies of God, that ye present your bodies a living sacrifice"[10] was the spirit of his pleadings. Having received mercy, he was an exponent of mercy. Having been delivered from his own prejudices, he was eager that all might find release from their destructive power.

How can we be so brazen as to be prejudiced against a

[8] Matthew 7:1.

[9] I Corinthians 13:4-7.

[10] Romans 12:1.

person when God in his mercy has been so merciful toward us?

THIRD: We can show mercy by *sharing the gospel of Christ* with others.

Man's spiritual poverty is even more wretched than his physical poverty. His failure to do what he ought to do and be what he ought to be proves that there is something inherently wrong with him.

The Bible puts it this way: "The heart is deceitful above all things, and desperately wicked."[11] All immorality, wantonness, greed, selfishness, prejudice, suffering, hatred, and bigotry stems from one source: the human heart. Nothing in the universe has fallen lower, and yet by the grace of God nothing can rise higher.

The fact that after two thousand years of Christianity more than half of the world's population knows nothing about the saving, transforming grace of Christ should stir us to a renewed dedication to tell a dying world about the mercy of God.

Jesus said: "Go ye into all the world, and preach the gospel to every creature."[12]

Notice the little word *go*. A little word—but world-wide in its sweep! The apostles had first *come*, and now Jesus commands them to *go!*

We have come in this generation and stopped short, but Christ says, "Go." A little word—but wrapped up in this little word is the whole sum and substance of Christ's gospel. It should be the watchword of every true follower of Christ. It should be emblazoned on the banners of the Church. "Go," says the Master. Nineteen hundred years have dragged their weary lengths down the road of time, and yet millions of people are sitting in spiritual darkness.

There are two conceptions of the condition of man's fallen nature. Some assert that human nature is radically good and may rise to its highest excellence independent of God. But the Christian declares that human nature is radically bad and the power to purify it and elevate it is in Christ—and Christ alone. The power to suppress vice and develop virtue is not

[11] Jeremiah 17:9.
[12] Mark 16:15.

65

in man nor of man—but outside of man, higher than man. It is in Christ.

However, today there are statesmen who assume that better organized human government is the remedy for the world's dilemma. They assume that inasmuch as vice and crime flow from ignorance and poverty that virtue could issue from knowledge and competence. Yet history proves that this theory is inadequate. Constitutional and statutory law lacks the essential element to purify human nature. The power is not within the province of law, whether human or divine.

The Bible says: "By the deeds of the law there shall no flesh be justified in His sight."[13] Again: "What the law could not do, in that it was weak . . . God sending his own Son in the likeness of sinful flesh . . . condemned sin in the flesh."[14]

All of us agree that one form of government may be better than another, but all forms of government have been inadequate to suppress vice and give universal prevalence to virtue. Rome was no more pure under the eloquent Cicero than under the cruel Nero.

History proves that, in their origin, vice and virtue lie beyond the reach and scope of civil law; and yet today there are many statesmen who believe that our type of democracy should be imposed upon nations throughout the world and that our type of democracy should be a "cure-all" for all the world's ills. So we have gone out to pagan nations, trying to westernize them when they were not prepared for it, trying to sell them on the idea that our kind of law was better than theirs.

Law can elevate society, but it cannot reach the principles from which our behavior springs. Back of constitutions, back of laws, back of administrations, there must be a moral code which is the power and glory of all human government.

Naturally, I believe that America has the greatest government in all the world. But our government is certainly going to fall like a rope of sand if unsupported by the moral sentiment of our people. Our moral sentiment in this country comes

[13] Romans 3:20.
[14] Romans 8:3.

from Christianity accepted and practiced in everyday life. When this Christianity disappears, the moral sentiment that shapes our nation's goal will disappear with it.

Then also, there is the scholar who claims that the remedy for vice is to be found in a universal system of education. His opinion is that man will be made pure and happy by intellectual culture and mental repose.

Suppose that education is the answer to all the problems that man faces. Develop the intellectual to the maximum; yet do you get virtue? Knowledge did not save Solomon from vice or Bryon from immorality. Art and education may refine the taste; but they cannot purify the heart, forgive sin, and regenerate the individual.

It is not simply education in civilization that the world is wanting today, but civilization with enlightened conscience; not simply railroads and steamships and gigantic corporations, but corporations and steamships free from graft and taint of every kind.

I would rather have a world filled with savages than with civilized fiends. Better the wild, unexplored wilderness than the debauched palace of civilized shame. Better the cannibal of the South Seas than the civilized vultures of our cities.

Would I drive out civilization? you ask. No, I would *reform* it *by regeneration*. I would starve out graft and put in honesty. I would drive out prejudice and put in the Golden Rule. I would drive out ruthlessness and put in mercy. This can be done only through an acceptance of Jesus Christ as personal Savior on the part of individuals who make up the society of the world.

You can put a public school and a university in the middle of every block of every city in America—but you will never keep America from rotting morally by mere intellectual education. Education cannot be properly called education which neglects the most important parts of man's nature. Partial education throughout the world is far worse than none at all if we educate the mind but not the soul.

Turn a half-educated man loose upon the world, put him in your community with inexhaustible resources at his command but recognizing no power higher than his own—he is a monstrosity! He is but halfway educated and is far more dangerous than if he were not educated at all. He is a speeding locomotive without an engineer. He is a tossing ship without a compass, pilot, or destiny.

To think of civilizing men without converting them to Christ is about as wise as to think about transforming wolves into lambs merely by washing them and putting on them a fleece of wool.

"Happy are the merciful: for they shall obtain mercy."

The mercy the world needs is the grace, love, and peace of our Lord Jesus Christ. It is His transforming and regenerating power that the world needs more than anything else.

To be sure, we are to use the world's physical resources, but along with them we are to take the regenerating power of Christ. We are to take a cup of cold water in one hand and regeneration in the other and give them to a physically and spiritually starved world. We have thought that man's needs were entirely physical, but we are beginning to realize that they are also spiritual.

The gospel of Christ provides for man's *physical being*. Materialism can see nothing in our bodies except laboratory analyses, but the Bible with stern rebuke exclaims: "What? know ye not that your body is the temple of the Holy Spirit?"[15]

The gospel provides for man's *intellect*. It stimulates his intellect to the highest activity. It commands the complete education of all his intellectual powers. The Bible instructs: "Gird up the loins of your mind."[16] It opens before a regenerated man a whole universe of truth.

The gospel also provides for man's *sensibilities*. "Let not your heart be troubled."[17] "Blessed are they that mourn: for they shall be comforted," says Jesus. This is what humanity needs. Humanity wants comfort in its sorrow, light in its darkness, peace in its turmoil, rest in its weariness, and healing in its sickness and diseases: the gospel gives all of this to man.

[15] I Corinthians 6:19.

[16] I Peter 1:13.

[17] John 14:1.

The gospel provides for man's *will*. It provides that man may yoke his will to the omnipotent will of God and thereby become omnipotent himself.

The gospel also provides for man's *moral nature*. Its code of morals is acknowledged by any man to be above reproach.

The gospel also provides the only satisfaction in the universe for man's *spiritual nature*. The gospel recognizes the tremendous fact of sin and proposes an adequate remedy.

It does not evade the age-old question "What must I do to be saved?" by saying there is no need of salvation. It does not lift a man out of the pit by telling him that he is not bad. It does not remove the sting of a man's conscience by taking away conscience itself. It does not haunt men.

The gospel shows men their wounds and bestows on them love. It shows them bondage and supplies the hammer to knock away their chains. It shows them nakedness and provides them the garments of purity. It shows them their poverty and pours into their lives the wealth of heaven. It shows them their sins and points them to the Savior.

This is the message we are to take to a lost, confused, and bewildered world! This is showing mercy!

There are those near you in your own community who need the regenerating power of Christ. You can call them by name. I suggest that you make a list and begin by spending time in prayer for them. Ask God to show you how to witness to them and how to win them. Their lives can be transformed by the message you give them. You are to share this gospel you have received. If Christ has done anything for you, then share it. In so doing, you are showing mercy!

As you have received the mercy of God by the forgiveness of sin and the promise of eternal life—thus you are to show mercy! And in showing mercy you will not only receive mercy but you will find a stimulating happiness!

VII

HAPPINESS THROUGH PURITY

"Blessed are the pure in heart:
for they shall see God."

The heart is considered in Scripture far more than a bodily organ. It is called the seat of the emotions. Fear, love, courage, anger, joy, sorrow, and hatred are ascribed to the heart. It has come to stand for the center of the moral, spiritual and intellectual life of a man. It is said to be the seat of a man's conscience and life.

Jesus said, "Happy are the pure in heart." Now, we should be able to take that for just what it means. If the heart is the seat of the affection, then our love toward God must be pure. If the heart is the center of our motives, then our motives must be pure. If the heart is the residence of our will, then our will must be yielded to Christ. We are to be pure in love, pure in motive, and pure in desire.

It might be well to pause at this point to observe just what is meant by being "pure in heart."

Did Jesus mean that we were to attain a sinless perfection, a spiritual state in which it would be impossible for us to fail again? No.

To be pure in heart does not mean that you must live in a straitjacket, looking pious and retreating into monastic seclusion. Jesus denounced the Pharisees because they had a false conception of heart purity. He said: "Woe unto you, scribes and Pharisees, hypocrites! for ye are like unto whited sepulchres, which indeed appear beautiful outward, but are within full of dead men's bones, and of all uncleanness."[1]

Jesus's debate with the Pharisees was right at this point.

[1] Matthew 23:27.

They avowed that the favor of God was gained by making clean the outside of the cup, by observing certain religious rites, and by keeping the letter of the law. In other words, they worked from the "outside in" rather than from the "inside out."

But this was not God's plan. This did not produce purity of heart. This did not bring about happiness of soul.

Their superficial religion was powerless to cleanse their hearts from their moral filth and corruption; hence the Pharisees were not happy men. They had furrowed brows, nervous tension, frustration. They were full of resentments, bitternesses, prejudices, and hatreds. Why? Simply because they had lost sight of God's conception of the pure in heart. They thought that as long as they kept the letter of the law that that was enough.

But Jesus taught that God looks deeper than the outside actions of an individual. He searches and ponders the heart. God judges not so much the outside as he does the inside. He looks to the motives, thoughts and intents of your heart.

I have a little daughter whom we call "Bunny." She is a sweet, loving, co-operative child. She is at the age where she is obsessed with the desire to help Daddy. Whatever I do, she says, "Daddy, let me help you." Now Bunny means well, but between you and me, she is seldom of any valuable assistance in a constructive way. If she helps me weed the flowers, she pulls up the flowers instead of the weeds. If she helps me unload the groceries, she invariably drops something of value and breaks it. If she helps me clean my study, she makes a mess of things in general. But Bunny's motive is good—she really wants to help. So I try to encourage this good, though undeveloped, trait. I try to judge Bunny's motives.

This is exactly what God does. He does not judge the superficial goodness or the superficial badness that we do. He goes deeper into the soul and probes as a surgeon! When God is through probing our hearts, he says: "The heart is deceitful above all things, and desperately wicked: who can know it?"[2]

When Jesus had finished probing the hearts of the people with whom he came in contact, He said: "Out of the heart of

[2] Jeremiah 17:9.

71

men proceed evil thoughts, adulteries, fornications, murders, thefts, covetousness, wickedness, deceit, lasciviousness, an evil eye, blasphemy, pride, foolishness."[3] Jesus taught that the human heart was far from God: darkened, unbelieving, blind, proud, rebellious, idolatrous, and stony. He taught that the human heart in its natural state is capable of any wickedness and any crime.

A teen-age boy was arrested in New York for having committed one of the most vicious murders of our time. His mother exclaimed, "But he is a good boy!" She had not stopped to realize that an unregenerate human heart is potentially capable of any crime.

That is the reason that many of the peace treaties which have been signed in human history have not been kept and war has ensued. These treaties have been signed in good faith, but they were signed on the basis of trusting the motives of the other party. They have been broken time after time and millions have died on the battlefields of the world because the human heart is deceitful and desperately wicked.

Our hearts are impure! As a result, we are filled with inner tension, pride, frustration, confusion, and a thousand and one other spiritual, mental, and physical ills. The very root of our lives is bad.

Jesus says we will never be completely and supremely happy until our hearts are pure.

But if we have bad hearts, what can we do about them? "Should we try to reform or improve our hearts in some way?" you ask.

Man—ever intent to live independently of God and his transforming grace—claims that environment, education, and right mental attitudes can change the heart and make it pure. "Put men in a wholesome atmosphere and they will be good," the argument goes.

Although this may sound perfectly logical—like a good many man-made theories—it simply will not hold water. Put an African baboon in a Boston drawing room, and how long will

[3] Mark 7:21, 22.

it take for him to act like a human being? "But that is twisting the argument," our humanist friends will object.

I think not! For we are dealing with the problem of nature as opposed to environment. The nature of an animal is affected by environment but can never be radically and essentially changed by it. An animal trainer may subdue that wild nature to a degree, but the baboon will always have the nature of a baboon, regardless of training and environment.

There are others who say that our mental attitude toward life needs to be changed: "If we *think* right, we *are* right." To them the problem of evil is a psychological one. "Think positively," they say. "As a man thinketh in his heart, so is he."

This is all very good, and I have a great deal of sympathy for those who are trying through psychological means to help bring about better mental attitudes. But this also gives encouragement to the people who say, "Goody, goody! We can help ourselves, just as we had always thought." The "do-it-yourself" rage is spreading everywhere, and people are being told that to be happy all they have to do is to think "happiness thoughts."

However, God says that our need is deeper-seated than the mind. He did not say, "Blessed are they who think happiness thoughts." He said: "Blessed are the pure in heart: for they shall see God."

This heart purity is not produced by mental suggestion, by environment or by education. It is a miracle wrought by God himself. The Bible says: "A new heart also will I give you, and a new spirit will I put within you: and I will take away the stony heart out of your flesh."[4]

Purity of heart is a result of a rebirth, a miracle, a new creation. As the Bible says: "Which were born, not of blood, nor of the will of the flesh, nor of the will of man, but of God."[5]

You need a cleansed, forgiven, justified, new heart! Such can be received only as an act of God on the ground of the death of Christ on the cross.

[4] Ezekiel 36:26.

[5] John 1:13.

A Sunday-school teacher once told a class of boys and girls that nothing was impossible with God. One little boy objected, saying that he knew one thing God could not do.

"And what could that be?" asked the astonished teacher.

"To see my sins through the blood of Jesus Christ," the youngster wisely answered.

When we have properly confessed and renounced our sins and by faith received Christ into our hearts, then we receive a new heart from God. Only then can we be called "pure in heart." Only then can we know the secret of happiness!

Again, I should like to emphasize that this is not an emotional experience, though emotion may be a factor. You may not "feel" that you have a new heart but accept the fact by faith. Faith goes beyond logic, rationalization, and understanding. You may not be able to accept intellectually all that has been said on these pages, but I challenge you to believe and accept by faith that which you cannot understand. There would be no need for faith if we could understand all about God.

Jesus insisted that we must become as little children before we could enter the kingdom of heaven. You must become as a little child and by faith grasp that which you cannot even altogether understand.

Certainly purity of heart is a prerequisite to entering the kingdom of heaven. There is no chance of a man's ever going to heaven until he has received purity of heart. This purity of heart comes as an act of God after you have renounced sin and received Christ!

Have you received a new heart? If you have, then you have found the beginning of the secret of happiness!

It is impossible to live pure lives until we have pure hearts. Many people today are trying to put the cart before the horse. They are teaching purity of motives, desires, and actions to old, deceitful hearts! No wonder we have ended up such moral failures in spite of our vaunted knowledge and psychological approaches. Pure motives, desires, and actions stem from pure hearts.

If you have received a cleansed and pure heart from God,

you are expected to live a pure life. Theologically (as we have already seen in the chapter on "Happiness Through Hunger and Thirst"), this is called "sanctification."

Pure hearts will be Christlike. It is God's desire that we be conformed to the image of His Son. If Christ lives within us and our bodies become the abode of the Holy Spirit, is it any wonder that we should be like Him?

The Bible says: "Let this mind be in you, which was also in Christ."[6] Jesus had a humble heart. If He abides in us, pride will never dominate our lives. Jesus had a loving heart. If He dwells within us, hatred and bitterness will never rule us. Jesus had a forgiving and understanding heart. If He lives within us, mercy will temper our relationships with our fellow men. Jesus had an unselfish heart. If He lives in us, selfishness will not predominate but service to God and others will come before our selfish interests.

You say, "That's a big order!" I admit that. It would be impossible if you had to measure up to Him in your own strength and with your natural heart.

Paul recognized that he could never attain this heart purity by his own striving. He said: "I can do all things *through* Christ which strengtheneth me."[7]

God hasn't left you alone, out on a limb! Jesus said to His disciples: "Lo, I am with you alway, even unto the end of the world."[8] They did what they did because He was with them. They were nothing but a group of rough, unlettered men; but with Christ in their hearts they "turned the world upside down."[9]

Christ provided the possibility of purity by his death on the cross. We have seen that the righteousness and the purity of God are imputed to men who confess their sins and receive Christ into their hearts.

Webster defines purity: "Freedom from foreign admixture or deleterious matter. Cleanness; freedom from foulness or

[6] Philippians 2:5.

[7] Philippians 4:13.

[8] Matthew 28:20.

[9] Acts 17:6.

dirt. Freedom from guilt or the defilement of sin; innocence; chastity. Freedom from any sinister or improper motives or views."

Though all of these ideas are embraced in the term *purity,* they do not set up an absolute standard by which to judge what is foreign and what is not, what is sin and what is not. It is perhaps best to regard purity in the all-embracing connotation: complete conformity to the holiness of God.

The Scriptures continually ask us to strive after *physical, mental,* and *moral* purity. God says: "Be ye holy; for I am holy."[10] Further the Scripture says that, without holiness, "no man shall see the Lord."[11] Again the Scripture says: "Who shall ascend into the hill of the Lord? or who shall stand in his holy place? He that hath clean hands, and a pure heart; who hath not lifted up his soul unto falsehood, nor sworn deceitfully."[12] We are actually commanded in Scripture: "Keep thyself pure."[13]

God wants us *to be pure in body.* This includes *physical cleanliness.*

Caverno says, "When one realizes that by uncleanness of person or property he may endanger the health or life of family or even of society about him—as in keeping conditions that develop typhoid fever—he begins to realize that there is a close tie between cleanliness and morals."

The ancient Jews strove for physical cleanliness on religious grounds; and although the Old Testament laws of purification have been abolished as detailed prescriptions for today, the principle of physical cleanliness is still in force.

Even in the poorest of circumstances a person can afford some soap and water. There is absolutely no excuse for a Christian's being unclean, unkempt, or slovenly. If you have a pure heart, you will also want to have a pure body.

Some time ago a man came to me testifying as to his religious experience, but I could hardly keep my mind on what

[10] I Peter 1:16.

[11] Hebrews 12:14.

[12] Psalm 24:3, 4.

[13] I Timothy 5:22.

he was saying because his "B.O." was so strong! I know a professing Christian who boasts about the fact that he takes a bath only once a week and can wear the same shirt two weeks without a change! This is a disgrace to the kingdom of God and indicates that there is something wrong with his purity of heart.

Being pure in body also includes *chastity*. Thus Paul says: "This is the will of God, even your sanctification, that ye should abstain from fornication . . ."[14]

How often the Scriptures warn against the sins of adultery and fornication. It is significant that in many references Paul mentions "uncleanness" immediately after "fornication."

Our newspapers are filled with stories of immorality in various parts of the nation: the stories of sex orgies in an eastern city where married couples exchanged wives and husbands for an evening . . . a story out of California, where teen-agers ganged up and forced women to submit to their perversions . . . a story is told of a non-virgin club in a high school in a southern city—in order to be a member, virginity had to be violated . . . we are told by sociological statisticians that the majority of men and women have had affairs before marriage . . . we are also told that one out of every four wives in this country is unfaithful to her husband, and that more than half of the husbands of America are unfaithful to their wives.

Let me warn you that the Scripture teaches that God hates immorality as much as, or more than, any other sin!

At the turning of the century a number of philosophies began to have popular acceptance with the American people. We are now beginning to feel the impact of their teaching. We are beginning to reap what we have sown. The names of Nietzsche and his philosophy of the coming superman, Sigmund Freud with his introduction to psychoanalysis, and the subjective theology of Schleiermacher were all the rage a few years ago. It is almost impossible to estimate the impact of their behavioristic philosophies.

Many have been convinced that the Bible is not God's reve-

14 I Thessalonians 4:3.

lation, that salvation is to come through man and not through Christ and that morality is relative and not absolute.

The practical results of this intellectual acceptance of humanism and behaviorism have been a degeneration of morals and the abandonment of religious ideals. The wave of behavioristic psychology that swept our college campuses and permeated the high school classrooms is now ingrained in the way our youth are living. Puritanical ideals are scorned, immorality is laughed out of school—"God is old-fashioned!" What else can we expect but that thousands of our young people are growing up to be immoral? The Bible warns time after time that no immoral nation can survive and no immoral individual shall enter the kingdom of God.

One of the Ten Commandments says: "Thou shalt not commit adultery."[15] I am keenly aware that this is a delicate subject and that it is usually considered taboo by clergymen. But the newspapers mention it, pornographic writers make it the theme of their writings, it is the theme of everyday gossip, children talk about it, and almost every magazine has discussions and pictures about it. And beyond all that, the Bible mentions it over and over again as one of the worst sins! So why in the name of all that is just, proper, and holy cannot preachers sound the warning against it?

The Bible says time after time: "Thou shalt not commit adultery." What does this word *adultery* mean? It is derived from the same Latin root from which we get our word *adulterate* which means "corrupt; to make impure or to weaken."

Sin is not merely the use of that which is corrupt, but more often the misuse of that which is pure and good. So adultery can apply to many things. This sin was so terrible that under Jewish law it was punishable by death. Under the Roman law it was punishable by death. Under the Greek law it was punishable by death. And under God's law, the Bible says, it is punishable by spiritual death.

The Bible says: "She that liveth in pleasure is dead while

[15] Exodus 20:14.

she liveth,"[16] and "The wages of sin is death."[17] The Bible says we are to keep our bodies pure, we are to abstain from fleshly lust. This sin is a sin not only against the body but against God.

God also wants us *to be pure in mind*.

"Whatsoever things are pure . . . think on these things."[18]

Returning to the question of chastity, we note that Jesus said: "Ye have heard that it was said . . . Thou shalt not commit adultery: But I say unto you, That whosoever looketh on a woman to lust after her hath committed adultery with her already in his heart."[19]

You can commit immorality *by evil imaginations*. In Genesis 6:5 we read: "And God saw that the wickedness of man was great in the earth, and that every imagination of the thoughts of his heart was only evil continually." God is concerned with your imaginations, for they in a large measure determine what kind of a person you are to be.

Solomon said: "As [a man] thinketh in his heart, so is he."[20] If your thoughts are evil, then your acts will be evil. If your thoughts are godly, then your life will be godly.

Robert Browning said: "Thought is the soul of the act." Emerson said: "Thought is the seat of action, the ancestor of every action is thought."

If God destroyed the world once for its continual evil imaginations, is it not reasonable to believe that all of the sin, lust, and licentiousness that is rampant today grieves His heart just as it did in that day?

Many people dream of sin, imagine sin, and if granted the opportunity would indulge in sin. All they lack is the occasion to sin. So in the sight of God they are sinners as great as though they had actually committed immorality.

All transgression begins with sinful thinking. You who have come to Christ for a pure heart, guard against the pictures

[16] I Timothy 5:6.

[17] Romans 6:23.

[18] Philippians 4:8.

[19] Matthew 5:27, 28.

[20] Proverbs 23:7.

of lewdness and sensuality which Satan flashes upon the screen of your imaginations, select with care the books you read, choose discerningly the kind of entertainment you attend, the kind of associates with whom you mingle, and the kind of environment in which you place yourself. You should no more allow sinful imaginations to accumulate in your mind and soul than you would let garbage collect in your living room.

Someone has said: "You cannot help the first look, but the second look is sin." Ask God to cleanse your mind and keep it purified. This can be done through reading the Bible, daily prayer, and association with the right kind of people.

As we have seen, Jesus indicated that you can commit immorality by a *look*. The Bible places the "lust of the eye" right along with other major sins. Listen: "For all that is in the world, the lust of the flesh, and the lust of the eyes, and the pride of life, is not of the Father, but is of the world."[21]

Peter spoke of having "eyes full of adultery."[22] No wonder Job said: "I made a covenant with my eyes; why then should I think upon a maid?"[23]

Your eyes see only what your soul allows it to see. If your heart is out of harmony with God and you have never been born again, the odds are that you will have a perverted, distorted view of life. Like Paul, the scales of lust and animal passion can fall from your eyes when you catch a vision of Christ. At this moment you can make a covenant with your eyes. Take your eyes and nail them to the cross until you can say, "They have been crucified with Christ, never again to lust."

Immorality can be committed by the *tongue*. The Scripture warns about evil communications that corrupt good manners. The Psalmist said: "Set a watch, O Lord, before my mouth."[24] Off-color jokes and dirty stories have no place in the Christian life. Thousands of people are committing immorality by the way they talk. Keep your talk pure. Ask God to purify your tongue.

[21] I John 2:16.
[22] II Peter 2:14.
[23] Job 31:1.
[24] Psalm 141:3.

You can commit immorality by the way you *dress*. If you women purposely dress to entice a man to sin, then you are guilty whether the act is committed or not. A girl said one day, "I came forward in your meeting and accepted Christ. A few nights later I was going to a party. I put on my dress. I looked in the mirror, and it seemed as though Jesus were looking at me. I went to my wardrobe and changed my dress. And now I dress as though Jesus were my escort each evening." Dress to please Christ—in all modesty and good taste. You can be smart, trim and in the latest fashion without having that "Hollywood look" that has become a damnation to this country.

You can commit immorality while *reading* unclean books and looking at unclean pictures. Our newsstands today are so indecent that a Christian cannot look upon them without blushing, and yet thousands of people are buying unclean literature and the wrong type of comic books. By feeding your lust, you are sinning against God.

Many of you who are reading these pages have committed this terrible sin of breaking the Seventh Commandment. You have been unfaithful to your wife or husband, or you young people have yielded to this temptation. You have become impure in regards to chastity.

Although the Bible teaches that this sin leads to hell, there is good news! The woman at the well had broken this commandment, but Christ forgave her and met the need of her life. Mary Magdalene had broken this commandment, but Christ wonderfully met the need of her life and cleansed her from sin. The sinful woman who had been taken in adultery was brought to Jesus by the Pharisees, but He said: "Neither do I condemn thee: go, and sin no more."[25] He did not condone her, but neither did He condemn her, because she had trusted in Him. He sent her away redeemed and forgiven. Christ will do the same for you if you will let Him.

Not only does God want us to be pure in body and pure in mind, but He wants us *to be pure in conduct*.

[25] John 8:11.

Paul says: "Let no corrupt communication proceed out of your mouth, but that which is good to the use of edifying, that it may minister grace unto the hearers."[26]

Jesus said to the Pharisees: "Ye generation of vipers, how can ye, being evil, speak good things? for out of the abundance of the heart the mouth speaketh. A good man out of the good treasure of the heart bringeth forth good things: and an evil man out of the evil treasure bringeth forth evil things. But I say unto you, That every idle word that men shall speak, they shall give account thereof in the day of judgment. For by thy words thou shalt be justified, and by thy words thou shalt be condemned."[27]

Cursing, telling smutty stories, vilifying the good name of another and referring irreverently to God and the Scriptures may be considered as coming under the expression *corrupt speech*. Our speech is to be clean, pure, and wholesome.

Under this rule of good conduct also come our associations. Paul says that evil companionships corrupt good morals. The Bible warns against being unequally yoked with unbelievers. This condemns all business, social, fraternal, and religious associations in which unchristian principles and practices govern. Concerning the latter, John says: "If there come any unto you, and bring not this doctrine, receive him not into your house, neither bid him God-speed: For he that biddeth him God-speed is partaker of his evil deeds."[28]

Christians who are in associations that are evil and corrupt are asked to "come out from among them, and be ye separate, and touch not the unclean thing."[29] God promises that if they do, He will receive them into His most intimate fellowship.

The Bible teaches that purity of conduct includes *truthfulness*. The Bible teaches that we should be truthful in our representations of ourselves. With what scorn Christ denounced the hypocrisy of the scribes and Pharisees! In the

[26] Ephesians 4:29.

[27] Matthew 12:34-37.

[28] II John 10, 11.

[29] II Corinthians 6:17.

Sermon on the Mount, He rebuked all hypocritical giving, praying, fasting, and correcting of others.

We should also be truthful in speaking of our past achievements in our particular vocation. God does not ask us to understate the facts—that might even be untruthfulness—but neither does He want us to overrate our achievements or our gifts, either in thought or in speech. A lie is anything contrary to the naked truth.

We are also to be truthful in our business affairs. All misrepresentations of the quality of our merchandise, all false weights and measures, all forging of checks and other legal papers, and all unjust alterations of accounts are sins of untruthfulness and indicate lack of purity. The farmer who puts his spoiled wheat between two layers of good wheat when he takes it to the market and the fruit grower who puts his best fruit on top in his measure are dishonest. The man who misrepresents an article that is subject to duty on entering the country and the taxpayer who does not supply all the desired information are dishonest.

Being pure in conduct also includes *honesty* and *integrity* in dealing with our fellow men. Employers in business are to give proper wages for work done, while employees are to put in a full hour's honest labor for the wages they receive. A Christian should be known in his neighborhood or place of business as an honest man, a man who can be trusted.

Jesus said: "Blessed are the pure in heart."

Do you want to be happy? All right, apply this Beatitude to your heart. Take it to yourself. The pure in heart are the only ones who can know what it means to be supremely happy. Their hearts are pure toward God and, as a result, are pure toward their fellow men.

They are happy because in possessing Him who is All and in All, they envy no man's worldly goods. They are happy because they envy not another man's praise or another man's place in the sun. Because they are the enemy of no man, they regard no man their enemy. The result is peace with God and the world. Because their sins have been freely forgiven, they freely forgive those who have wronged them. They are thus purged of contemptuous malice.

But the greatest happiness that comes to the pure in heart is not only a proper relationship with men but a sublime relationship with God. "For they shall see God." The gates of Eden swing open once more. God and man walk together once again.

The secret of happiness is God! The secret of seeing and knowing God is a pure heart . . . a pure heart comes from God! Get a pure heart, and you can be supremely happy—no matter what the circumstances!

VIII.

HAPPINESS THROUGH PEACEMAKING

"Blessed are the peacemakers:
for they shall be called the children of God."

The problem of human strife is as old as man. It had its beginning on the outskirts of Eden when Cain, driven by envy, murdered his more devout brother, Abel. Men fought then as now: primarily because strife was inherent in their natures.

Professor Quincy Wright, in *A Study of War,* shows that in the 461 years from 1480 to 1941 the various nations experienced wars as follows: Great Britain 78 wars, France 71, Spain 64, Russia 61, Austria 52, Germany 23, China 11, Japan 9; the United States 13, and, in addition, 110 wars were fought, often ruthlessly, against the Indians within the United States.

Someone has pointed out that in the past four thousand years there has been less than three hundred years of peace. Even the most optimistic person is forced to admit that there is something seriously wrong with a world that has such a passion for destruction.

If a man were sent from Mars to report earth's major business, he would in all fairness have to say that war was the earth's chief industry. He would report that the nations of the world were vying with each other in a race to see which could make deadlier weapons and amass bigger armies. He would say that earth's people are too quarrelsome to get along with each other and too selfish to live peacefully together.

But why is it that after these thousands of years of life on this planet we are no nearer peace than were the warring tribes of ancient history?

The simple fact is: there can be no real peace in the world until we have peace with God.

Meaningless mouthings about peace will not bring it to the world. Last May Day in Glasgow we watched the Communists march around St. George's Square carrying their banners with the words: "Our motto is PEACE!" My thoughts raced back to Korea, where I had seen with my own eyes the havoc and suffering caused by these very people who now use *peace* as their motto.

Peace is more than five little white letters painted on a piece of red cloth, carried by a goose-stepping zealot in a Red parade. It is not a mere cessation of hostilities, a momentary halt in a hot or cold war. Rather, it is something positive. It is a specific relationship with God into which a person is brought. It is a spiritual reality in a human heart which has come into vital contact with the Infinite God.

The Bible says: "But now in Christ Jesus ye who sometimes were far off are made nigh by the blood of Christ. For He is our peace, who hath made both one."[1]

I saw a painting in England which showed a soldier who had gone to the front to repair the communications lines. The message which was to flow through those lines meant life to hundreds and perhaps thousands of men. He found a breach in the wires but had nothing with which to repair the break. While the enemy shells were bursting around him, he took one broken cable in his left hand and stretching his right hand grasped the other cable and made the connection. The dramatic picture had a one-word title: "Through."

Christ, in His vicarious death on the cross, repaired the breach between God and man. The Bible says: "He is our Peace."[2] Those who were afar off are made nigh . . . He has made both one.

Although God has never been an enemy of man, man by choice became an enemy of God. The revolt began in the Garden of Eden, when Adam revolted from God and allied himself with Satan. It was there that the enmity began. It was there

[1] Ephesians 2:13, 14.
[2] Ephesians 2:14.

that the abysmal breach was made by man, by deliberate choice.

The history of man has been the record of a futile effort to live happily and peacefully apart from God. When Israel turned from the worship of Jehovah to the worship of idols, she lost her peace, and either fell a prey to other nations or entered a series of wars. Any step away from the true, living God is a step in the direction of strife.

Hitler felt pretty sure of himself when he denounced the Bible and Christianity and tried to create a "pure Nordic" church with a god who bore a striking resemblance to Thor or Woden, the war gods. We are all acquainted with the record of what happened in Germany. A regime which on the surface looked strong enough to conquer the world crumbled and fell swiftly. Today we see a new Germany emerging out of the rubble of World War II, but it is a more reverent Germany, wherein many eyes are searching the heavens for the true and living God. In our tour of Germany we felt the heart-hunger of these gifted and virile people for a faith which brings peace and not war.

Jesus said: "Blessed are the peacemakers: for they shall be called the children of God."

Where does peacemaking begin? How can we become peacemakers?

We have pointed out that peace can never come out of war. War is the sire of poverty, depression, suffering, and hatred—but it has never given us permanent peace.

Can peace be discovered within ourselves? Freud has told us that peace is but a mental attitude. Cast off our phobias, shed our neuroses, and "bingo!"—we'll have the coveted peace men long for.

I respect psychiatry for what it can do. Unquestionably it has helped many. But it certainly is no satisfactory substitute for the peace which can come only from God. If psychiatry leaves God out, ultimately we shall see psychiatrists going to each other for treatment. There can be no peace until we find peace with God. The Bible says: "He is our peace."[3]

[3] Ephesians 2:14.

The Bible is not content to leave the nature of the peace Christ purchased for us in doubt. It sketches that peace in the clearest of outlines. Christ made peace by the blood of his cross.[4] He bore the sins of men, so those who know His saviorhood need be troubled by them no longer. He interposed Himself between doomed men and the wrath of God. And He stands still between the Holy God and fallen man in his strife, rebellion, conflict. He is the only hope for peace in the inner spiritual warfare of the soul, and for that reason also is the only hope for social stability.

In a materialistic world which has tried to sever diplomatic relations with God, we have nowhere to retreat except within ourselves. We are like turtles in a traffic jam—the best we can do is to pull our heads into our shells and shut our eyes. But that's a good way to get the life crushed out of you, as any dead turtle can attest.

If we are to be peacemakers, we first must make our peace with God.

The Bible says: "There is no peace, saith the Lord, unto the wicked."[5] Isaiah said: "The way of peace they know not; and there is no judgment in their goings: they have made them crooked paths; whosoever goeth therein shall not know peace."[6]

Man's conflict with man has been but an expression on the human level of his conflict against God. Until man finds an armistice with God, he cannot know peace with his fellow man. Both ancient and modern men have discovered the peace of God. David said: "I will both lay me down in peace, and sleep: for thou, Lord, only makest me dwell in safety."[7]

A former pagan, having recently discovered the peace of God, said to me the other day, "My wife and I used to wake up in the morning quarreling and go to bed at night bickering —but since we have found peace with God, our home is a heaven on earth."

[4] Colossians 1:20.
[5] Isaiah 48:22.
[6] Isaiah 59:8.
[7] Psalm 4:8.

You can have peace with God! "But how can I discover this peace?" you ask.

The first step in finding peace with God is to stop fighting Him. Through the Bible, through the church, through the lives of Christian people, God has been trying to get through to you for years with the message that He wants to give you peace. Christ said to his disciples: "My peace I give unto you."[8] He is no respecter of persons—He wants to give you peace, too. But He can't give you His peace as long as you lift high the red flag of rebellion. You must stop resisting God! You must no longer shut Him out of your life! You must stop fighting! You must give up!

The second step in finding peace with God is to surrender to Him. Lay down your weapons of war! Get off the offensive, and stop *being* offensive! The Bible says regarding a people who had no peace with God: "Be ye not stiffnecked, as your fathers were, but yield yourselves unto the Lord."[9]

When you surrender to a "friendly enemy"—to one who loves you—you are using good sense.

The peace which follows the acceptance of Christ as Savior is more than earthly peace, and it is the greatest of spiritual treasures even though it may not always bring worldly prosperity with it. To know Christ is to have the supremest of riches, a place in the kingdom of God. And men and women who give Him first place find that there is no need for anxiety about this world's goods. "Seek ye first the kingdom of God . . . and all these things shall be added unto you."[10]

But there is one more aspect of this peace with God. It is not just a passive peace which sits idly under a willow tree strumming a harp. It is a peace of activity and service.

The third step in finding peace with God is to serve him. The Bible told an ancient people who sued for peace, not only

[8] John 14:27.
[9] II Chronicles 30:8.
[10] Matthew 6:33.

to yield but to "serve the Lord your God, that the fierceness of his wrath may turn away from you."[11]

How do we find peace with God? We must stop fighting! We must surrender! We must serve! Of course these steps will be motivated by faith and mingled with love.

Having found peace *with* God, next we experience the peace *of* God. God does not consider us slaves but sons. The Bible says: "Beloved, now are we the sons of God."[12] Having yielded to Him, we are led into the lush vineyards of His grace and made partakers of the fruit of the Spirit.

To all who surrender to Him and serve Him, He gives the Holy Spirit, the Spirit of peace. This is the Spirit with whom our Lord and the disciples were baptized. This is the Spirit who enabled Christ to say: "Forgive them; for they know not what they do."[13] This was the Spirit who caused Stephen even in the midst of stonings to pray: "Lord, lay not this sin to their charge."[14] This was the Spirit who enabled all of the disciples save one—who proved himself no real disciple—to die uncomplainingly for their Lord. They could do this only because they had the peace of God.

This peace of God is not a mere abstraction advocated by preachers and theologians. Thousands can witness that they have actually experienced the peace of God and have found it wonderfully adequate for this present day.

Some time ago a Christian workman was fatally injured when he fell from a high scaffolding on a construction job. A minister was called, and when he saw the serious condition of the man, he said, "My dear man, I'm afraid you're dying. I exhort you, make your peace with God!"

"Make my peace with God, sir!" said the man, "Why, that was made nineteen hundred years ago when my glorious Savior paid all my debt upon the cruel tree. Christ *is* my peace, and I do know God—I *do* know God!"

[11] II Chronicles 30:8.
[12] I John 3:2.
[13] Luke 23:34.
[14] Acts 7:60.

You, too, can experience the peace of God through Christ: "For He is our peace."[15]

To have peace *with* God and to have the peace *of* God is not enough. This vertical relationship must have a horizontal outworking, or our faith is in vain. Jesus said that we were to love the Lord with all our hearts and our neighbor as ourselves. This dual love for God and man is like the positive and negative poles of a battery—unless both connections are made, we have no power. A personal faith is useless unless it has a social application.

I once saw a cartoon of a man rowing a boat toward a golden shore labeled "heaven." All around him were men and women struggling in vain to reach the shore and safety, but he was heedless of their peril. He was singing, "I am bound for heaven, hallelujah!" That is not an adequate picture of the Christian life.

If we have the peace *of* God and peace *with* God, we will become peacemakers. We will not only be at peace with our neighbors, but we will be leading them to discover the source of true peace in Christ.

Christianity increases the scope and area of our lives. It takes us from self-centeredness to multi-centeredness. Conversion takes us from introversion to extroversion.

Our lives take on new dimensions when we find peace with God. To explain this in simpler terms, let us visualize a right triangle setting on its horizontal base. At the apex or highest point in this triangle write the letter "G," representing God. At the point where the perpendicular line meets the base write the letter "Y," representing you. Then, at the opposite end of the horizontal line write the letter "O," which represents others. There, in geometric form, you have a visual diagram of our relationship with God and man. Our lives (which before we found the peace of God were represented by a single dot of self-centeredness) now take in an area in vital contact with two worlds. Peace flows down from God and out to our fellow

[15] Ephesians 2:14.

men. We become merely the conduit through which it flows. But there is peace in being just a "channel."

There are many areas of our lives where we can be peacemakers. There is no part of our lives which is not affected by this peace of God which we are to share with others.

FIRST: We can be peacemakers in the *home.*

In a complicated, mechanized age, it is no easy matter to keep the domestic life on an even keel. Modern gadgets, modern transportation and modern social changes have all but revolutionized our domestic life. Father goes to the club, mother to the bridge party, and junior to the teen canteen. The old-fashioned taffy pulls, family get-togethers and family altars seem to have gone out with the horse and buggy.

Even though the divorce rate is slightly diminishing in America, yet the home—which is the basic unit of our social structure—continues to disintegrate at an alarming rate. The breaking of the marriage vow is having an effect upon our other social institutions. A chain reaction has set in that could ultimately destroy the nation.

In the marriage ceremony, after the vows are said, the minister solemnly and reverently remarks: "What God hath joined together let no man put asunder." Is not God the party of the third part in a marriage? Should He not be taken into account in the marriage and in the home that emerges from that marriage? If God joins the couple together at the outset, should not His Presence be recognized in the home continually?

Many homes are on the rocks today because God has been left out of the domestic picture. With the continual clash of personalities in a domestic pattern, there must be an integrating force, and the Living God is that Force!

Mr. B came to me with a serious domestic problem. He and his wife quarreled violently over trifles. Each blamed the other for these orgies and the domestic stress had built up to the breaking point. I asked him a question to which I already knew the answer, "Mr. B, do you and your wife go to church, and do you have family prayer?" He answered that they did neither.

"Your trouble in the home, Mr. B," I said, "is the reflection of your lack of peace with God. Get right with God, and you'll be right with your wife!"

Mr. B did just that. In sincere repentance he confessed his sin to God, and I saw his facial expression change as the peace of Christ came into his heart. The light in his face mirrored the new glow in his soul. A few days later he led his wife to Christ. That home is now a happy one, for Christ is the head of that house.

Many couples think that if they have a better home, get a better job, or live in a different neighborhood that their domestic life will be happier. No! The secret of domestic happiness is to let God, the party of the third part in the marriage contract, have His rightful place in the home. Make peace with Him, and then you can be a real peacemaker in the home.

SECOND: We can be peacemakers in the *community*.

Our society is shot through with slander, libel, and gossip. The strife in many communities is almost unbearable. Here again, the basic cause is a faulty relationship to God.

The Bible says: "The works of the flesh are . . . hatred, variance . . . wrath, strife, seditions . . . envyings."[16] True, we find some of these in the first-century community of Christians. Yet "Behold, how they love one another" was the remark of those who observed the unique peace of the Christian society.

How can you be a peacemaker in your community?

The formula is simple: first, make your own peace with God, and then you can make peace in the community. The fruit of human nature is discord and bickering; "but the fruit of the Spirit is love, joy, peace, long-suffering, gentleness, goodness, faith, meekness, temperance."[17]

Our trouble is that we have tried to build a good society without God. We have in many localities taken the Bible out of our schools and God out of our conversation. The result is that decency has gone from the community, and bedlam reigns. Peace and decorum will be restored when the individuals in the community give God his proper place once more.

[16] Galatians 5:19-21.
[17] Galatians 5:22, 23.

THIRD: We can be peacemakers in the *church*.

We might as well face it: strife has even infiltrated our church life. It is true enough that the Church is now the Church militant. But as such its warfare ought to be that of dedication to revealed truth and divine holiness, and not intramural bickering and carnal disputes.

We read in the second chapter of Luke that Joseph and Mary lost Jesus one day. Where did they lose Him? They lost Him in the most unlikely place in all the world—in the temple. Passing strange, I know! But, I have seen many people lose Jesus right in church. I have seen them lose Him in a dispute about who was to be choir director, who was to play the organ, who was to be an elder, or who was to be the minister. Yes, because we are human, though Christian, it is easy to lose sight of Jesus right in the temple!

I know of two deacons who had quarreled over an old line fence, and they had not spoken to each other for a long time. One of them, wanting to make peace, took his Bible and went to visit his neighbor. Handing his Bible to his "old enemy," he said, "John, you read and I'll pray. We must be friends."

But John, fumbling for his glasses, said, "But I can't read. I haven't my spectacles."

"Take mine," said his peace-loving neighbor.

After they had read the Word and prayed together, they arose and embraced each other. John handed back the spectacles to his neighbor and said through his tears, "Jim, that old line fence looks different through your glasses."

When we have the peace of God, we can see things through "the other man's glasses," and by doing that we can make peace.

FOURTH: We can be peacemakers at *work*.

One of the greatest points of tension in our economy is the labor-management relationship. Many industries today are recognizing that disputation is costly on the part of both labor and management and are seeking industrial peace through God and faith in Him.

One minister wrote us the other day and said that he was chaplain in three industrial plants in Indiana. The managers

94

had found that if they sat down with their employees and listened to the Christian message once each day that everyone was in a better frame of mind.

In London, an industrialist gave his heart to Christ. He wrote us that he now conducts a chapel service in his plant and that two hundred attend the service regularly. "Never has there been more peace in our factory," he wrote.

Would you like to be an industrial peacemaker? You can be one—whether manager or laborer—if you make your peace with God first, and then seek by His grace to impart this peace to others.

When an employer and employees really know Christ, the lie is given to the Marxist thesis that all religion is the working man's opiate. To know Christ is to have part in His savior-hood and lordship of life. Godlier employers and godlier employees will find that the right makes a claim upon every life. Where the employer is Christ's servant and the employee is the employer's spiritual partner, they are linked in an eternal vocation.

We need peacemakers on the *international scene,* also.

When I watched President Eisenhower kneel in a chapel in Geneva before the Big Four Conference and ask God for divine guidance in the deliberations to follow, I felt sure that God would answer his earnest prayer. I believe that He did, for President Eisenhower during those days displayed the spirit of a true peacemaker on the international level. Kind, considerate of the opposition's viewpoint, and given to intelligent discussion, he emerged the undisputed hero of the Geneva Conference. Not because he held a "big stick" but because he convinced the Communists, at least in a measure, that he wanted peace and not war.

I am not a pure pacifist on the international scene any more than I am in our local community. Law and the enforcement of law, whether local or national, is both Biblical and logical. Police must use force to protect the community from evil men.

We should be vastly more interested in getting to the core of the problem of the criminal than we are in punishing him.

Punishment of a criminal, although necessary for the common good, seldom reforms him. Wars waged against an aggressor, in the common good of nations, is more a protection than it is a correction. In a sinless society it would not exist.

The only corrective measure in establishing peace is for men as individuals to know the peace of God. Though I am not wholly averse to movements which strive in one way or another for world peace, I have a strong conviction that such peace will never come unless there is a spiritual dynamic at the core. I pray for wars to cease just as I pray for crime to stop; but I know that the basic cause of both crime and war is the inherent sinfulness of human nature.

When Jesus told Nicodemus that he "must be born again," He was addressing not only a great teacher but all of us, for He saw in him a typical representative of the race. The world cannot be reborn until men are born again and are at peace with God.

Arnold Toynbee, the historian, says in line with this: "The West has erred because it has chosen to fight Communism with Communism's own material weapons. As long as the battle is fought on these terms, the Communists will keep on winning. The West must base its appeal on more than freedom, more than prosperity; it must base its appeal on religion. Only in this way can democracy turn the tables on the Communist assailants. The grace of God might bring about this miracle."

In regard to racial peace, let me say that for true Christians there is no race problem! The ground is level at the cross and there are no second-rate citizens with God. Admittedly, the problems are great, and will not be solved overnight; but if all people concerned will make sure that they have made their peace with God, it will then be a simpler matter to make peace with each other. If we approach the problem with a vindictive, intolerant, and unchristian attitude, we are destined to failure and disaster.

Peace-making is a noble vocation. But you can no more make peace in your own strength than a mason can build a wall without a trowel, a carpenter build a house without a hammer or an artist paint a picture without a brush. You must have the proper equipment. To be a peacemaker, you must know the Peace Giver. To make peace on earth, you must know the peace of heaven. You must know Him who "*is* our peace."

Jesus didn't leave a material inheritance to his disciples. All he had when he died was a robe, which went to the Roman soldiers; his mother, whom he turned over to His brother John; his body, which he gave to Joseph of Arimathea; and his spirit, which returned to his Father.

But He willed His followers something more valuable than gold, more enduring than vast land holdings and more to be desired than palaces of marble—He willed us His peace. He said: "My peace I give unto you: not as the world giveth, give I unto you. Let not your heart be troubled, neither let it be afraid."[18]

Only as we know Him and the peace He imparts can we be peacemakers . . . and He promised happiness to a maker of peace!

[18] John 14:27.

IX

HAPPINESS IN THE
MIDST OF PERSECUTION

*"Blessed are they which are persecuted
for righteousness' sake: for
theirs is the kingdom of heaven."*

Who wants to be persecuted? Our natural eyes can see no happiness in persecution. No one enjoys being maligned. Almost everyone wants the good will of his neighbors, and it is difficult to see what blessedness there could be in the enmity of one's fellow men.

Offhand, it would seem that being a Christian would elicit the admiration and acclaim of those about us. Christianity usually means that kindness, honesty, and unselfishness are included in the business of living. So it would seem that it would be in order to gather around a person whose life was dedicated to Christ and join in singing "For He's a Jolly Good Fellow, Which Nobody Can Deny."

It would seem so! But such is not the case. And it is good that this Beatitude gives us the occasion to sit down and rethink this age-old question: "Why are good people persecuted?"

No doubt you have asked yourself this question many times, and you have concluded, as have others, that there is usually something wrong with folk who are persecuted for righteousness' sake, that there is some quirk in their disposition, some personality peculiarity or some religious fanaticism which causes others to mistreat them. No, that is not always, or let us say that is not usually, the case.

Here is a spiritual law which is as unchangeable as the law of gravity: "All that will live godly in Christ Jesus shall suffer persecution."[1]

We must get this fact firmly fixed in our minds: we live in an

[1] II Timothy 3:12.

98

upside-down world. Men hate when they should love, men quarrel when they should be friendly, men fight when they should be peaceful, men wound when they should heal, men steal when they should share, men do wrong when they should do right.

I once saw a toy clown with a weight in its head. No matter what position you put it in, it invariably assumed an upside-down position. Put it on its feet or on its side, and when you let go it flipped back on its head.

Man in his unregenerate state is just like that! Do what you may with him, and he always reverts to an upside-down position. From childhood to maturity we are always prone to do what we should not do and to refrain from doing what we ought to do. That is our nature. We have too much weight in the head and not enough ballast in our hearts, so we flip upside down when left alone.

That is why the disciples to the world were misfits. To an upside-down man, a right-side-up man seems upside down. To a sinner, a righteous man is an oddity and an abnormality. A Christian's goodness is a rebuke to his wickedness; his being right side up is a reflection upon the worldling's inverted position. So the conflict is a natural one. Persecution is inevitable.

When Christ's disciples began to rearrange the world, certain lewd fellows cried in consternation, "These that have turned the world upside down are come hither also."[2] Herein lies the fundamental reason for Christian persecution. Christ's righteousness is so revolutionary and so contradictory to man's manner of living that it invokes the enmity of the world.

If we could assume that men were basically upright, then it would be the popularly accepted thing to "live godly in Christ Jesus."[3] But as long as Satan is loose in the world and men's hearts are dominated by his evil passions, it will never be easy or popular to be a follower of Christ.

Persecution is inevitable to those who are pilgrims and strangers in an alien land.

The Bible says: "But ye are a chosen generation, a royal

[2] Acts 17:6.

[3] II Timothy 3:12.

priesthood, a holy nation, a peculiar people; that ye should show forth the praises of him who hath called you out of darkness into his marvelous light: which in time past were not a people, but are now the people of God: which had not obtained mercy, but now have obtained mercy. Dearly beloved, I beseech you as strangers and pilgrims . . ."[4]

Aliens are rarely shown the "welcome mat." They are often accepted only with a tongue-in-cheek attitude. Being aliens, with our citizenship not in the world but in heaven, we as Christ's followers will inevitably be treated as "peculiar people" and as strangers.

Our life is not of this world. "Our citizenship is in heaven."[5] Our interests, primarily, are not in this world. Jesus said: "Lay up for yourselves treasures in heaven . . . for where your treasure is, there will your heart be also."[6] Our hope is not in this world. The Bible says: "We look for the Savior, the Lord Jesus Christ: Who shall change our vile body, that it may be fashioned like unto his glorious body, according to the working whereby he is able even to subdue all things unto himself."[7]

Hence, in every sense we are an enigma to the world. Like a few right-handed persons among a host of left-handed persons, we comprise a threat to their status quo. We cramp their style. We are labeled as "wet blankets," as kill-joys and as prudes. Like the enemies of Jesus, the world will always inquire contemptuously, "Art not thou also one of his disciples?"[8]

There will be times when the eyes of suspicion will be upon us, because, with men's hearts as they are, they cannot conceive of anyone wanting to live selflessly. Unbelievers will say we have "something up our sleeve," that we have a motive in being so righteous, that it is all a game, that it is sheer hypocrisy. The cry of "counterfeit!" follows the Christian's sincere efforts.

[4] I Peter 2:9-11.

[5] Philippians 3:20.

[6] Matthew 6:20.

[7] Philippians 3:20, 21.

[8] John 18:25.

Still another reason for persecution is that there is a war in progress.

The Word of God indicates this! The Bible says: "Fight the good fight of faith, lay hold on eternal life."⁹ Again: "No man that warreth entangleth himself with the affairs of this life; that he may please him who hath chosen him to be a soldier."¹⁰

The world, the flesh, and the devil are our enemies. In times of war one can hardly expect the good will of the enemy's forces. Though our weapons are not earthly, the enemy's weapons are earthly, and we can expect Satan to use every tool at his command for our persecution and destruction. War atrocities *will* be committed. They who live godly in Christ *shall* suffer persecution.

All life is a struggle—that is the nature of things. Even within our physical bodies, doctors tell us, a conflict for supremacy is going on. The bacteria in our blood stream is waging a constant war against alien germs. The red corpuscles fight the white corpuscles constantly in an effort to maintain life within the body.

A battle is also raging in the spiritual realm. The Bible says: "We wrestle not against flesh and blood, but against principalities, against powers, against the rulers of the darkness of this world, against spiritual wickedness in high places."¹¹

"We fight," the Bible says, "against the rulers of the darkness of this world." Darkness hates light.

> *Must I be carried to the skies,*
> *On flowery beds of ease;*
> *While others fought to win the prize,*
> *And sailed through bloody seas?*

I have a dog that would rather dig up a moldy carcass to chew on than to have the finest, cleanest meal. He can't help it—that is his nature.

Men cannot help that it is their nature to respond to the lewd,

⁹ I Timothy 6:12.
¹⁰ II Timothy 2:4.
¹¹ Ephesians 6:12.

the salacious, and the vile. They will have difficulty doing otherwise until they are born again. And until they *are* changed by the power of Christ, they will likely be at enmity against those who are associated with Christ.

And, finally, Jesus said that a cross is the Christian's lot.

"He that taketh not his cross, and followeth after me, is not worthy of me."[12]

Does this mean that we are to wear a symbol of the cross around our necks or on the lapel of our coats? Or does it mean that we are literally to carry a wooden cross?

No! It means that the reproach of Christ's cross, which he carried when he was in the world, is ours to carry now. Being at "cross-purposes" with the world is part and parcel of the Christian life. We should not covet nor expect the praise of ungodly men. On the contrary, we should expect their enmity. The very fact that they are inclined to persecute us is proof that we are "not of the world," that we are "in Christ." All of the persecution, all of the blasphemy, all of the railing that they would heap on Christ, they hurl against us. He took the reproach of the cross for us; now, it is ours to take it for Him.

As Paul said: "God forbid that I should glory, save in the cross of our Lord Jesus Christ, by whom the world is crucified unto me, and I unto the world."[13] This, Paul considered a privilege—the privilege of persecution. In that he gloried, because in a small way he was allowed to share in the sufferings of Christ.

Now, let us remember that this Beatitude says: "Blessed are they which are persecuted for righteousness' sake . . . when men shall revile you, and persecute you, and shall say all manner of evil against you falsely. . . ."[14]

Many times we suffer because of our own poor judgment, stupidity and blundering. There is no blessedness in this. I have known professed Christians who were dominated by bad dispositions, snap judgments, and poor manners and thought that people were opposed to them because of their "righteous-

[12] Matthew 10:38.

[13] Galatians 6:14.

[14] Matthew 5:10, 11.

ness." It was not their goodness which people resented—it was their lack of it.

We must be careful not to behave offensively, preach offensively, and dress offensively, and, when people are offended and shun us, blame it on the "offense of the cross." Our personal offensiveness is no credit to the gospel we preach.

Shabby Christians are poor advertisements for Christianity. Paul said: "We . . . suffer reproach, because we trust in the living God . . . but be thou an example of the believers, in word, in conversation, in charity, in spirit, in faith, in purity."[15] The reproach we experience is the natural resentment in the hearts of men toward all that is godly and righteous. This is the cross we are to bear. This is why Christians are often persecuted.

We have considered the reasons for Christians being persecuted. Now let us see what happiness and blessedness there is in persecution.

Our Lord promises that the persecuted will be happy. "Rejoice," He said, "and be exceeding glad: for great is your reward in heaven; for so persecuted they the prophets which were before you."[16]

The word *joy* has all but disappeared from our current Christian vocabulary. One of the reasons is that we have thought that joy and happiness were found in comfort, ease, and luxury. James did not say, "Count it all joy when you fall into an easy chair," but he said, "Count it all joy when you fall into divers temptations."[17]

The persecuted are happy because they are being processed for heaven. Persecution is one of the natural consequences of living the Christian life. It is to the Christian what "growing pains" are to the growing child. No pain, no development. No suffering, no glory. No struggle, no victory. No persecution, no reward!

The Bible says: "The God of all grace, who hath called us unto his eternal glory by Christ Jesus, after that ye have suffered a while, make you perfect, stablish, strengthen, settle

15 I Timothy 4:10, 12.

16 Matthew 5:12.

17 James 1:2.

you."[18] It is so easy to forget that "all things work together for good to them that love God."[19]

I have a friend who during the depression lost a job, a fortune, a wife, and a home. But he tenaciously held to his faith —the only thing he had left. One day he stopped to watch some men doing stonework on a huge church. One of them was chiseling a triangular piece of stone.

"What are you going to do with that?" asked my friend.

The workman said, "See that little opening away up there near the spire. Well, I'm shaping this down here so it will fit in up there."

Tears filled his eyes as he walked away, for it seemed that God had spoken through the workman to explain his ordeal through which he was passing, "I'm shaping you down here so you'll fit in up there."

After you have "suffered a while, make you perfect . . . settle you," echo the words from the Bible.

The persecuted for "righteousness' sake" are happy because they are identified with Christ. The enmity of the world is tangible proof that we are on the right side, that we are identified with our blessed Lord. He said that our stand for Him would arouse the wrath of the world. "And ye shall be hated of all men for my name's sake: but he that endureth to the end shall be saved."[20]

Christ, in a sense, is King in exile, and we who are His followers are often looked upon with derision. To be identified with Him here and now quite naturally entails some "loss of face," some persecution; but some day, we are told, we shall be "kings and priests" and shall be active participators in His kingdom.

Paul must have had this fact in mind when he said: "For I reckon that the sufferings of this present time are not worthy to be compared with the glory which shall be revealed in us.

[18] I Peter 5:10.
[19] Romans 8:28.
[20] Matthew 10:22.

For the earnest expectation of the creature waiteth for the manifestation of the sons of God."[21]

If we should be called upon to suffer all our lives, it would not be long compared to eternity. We are in the position of heirs to a large estate who gladly endure a few days of suffering and privation with the hope that we shall soon come into our fabulous inheritance. Such a glorious hope hangs a halo over the drab existence of the here and now.

Life cannot lose its zest when down underneath our present discomfort is the knowledge that we are children of a King. Complaining becomes foolish; behaving in the manner of the world is unworthy; and love, gentleness, and meekness become the hallmark of God's nobility. "All things" are taken in stride; burdens become blessings in disguise; every wound, like good surgery, is for our good; and etched in every cross is the symbol of a crown.

And last, persecution is blessed because it forms a dark backdrop for the radiance of the Christian life.

All the masterpieces of art contain both light and shadow. A happy life is not one filled only with sunshine, but one which uses both light and shadow to produce beauty. The greatest musicians as a rule are those who know how to bring song out of sadness. Fanny Crosby, her spirit aglow with faith in Christ, saw more with her sightless eyes than most of us do with normal vision. She has given us some of the great gospel songs which cheer our hearts and lives.

Paul and Silas sang their song of praise at midnight in a rat-infested jail in Philippi to the accompaniment of the jailer's whip. But their patience in suffering and persecution led to the heathen warden's conversion. The blood of the martyrs is mixed well into the mortar which holds the stones of civilization together.

The self-sacrifice of God's gentry through the centuries has contributed immeasurably to our culture, to our ethics and to our faith. Down deep we know that there are still things worth

[21] Romans 8:18, 19.

dying for, that an existence void of faith is still a fate worse than death.

O children of God, despair not at your suffering and persecution. In the words of Thornton Wilder: "Without your wounds, where would your power be that sends your low voice trembling into the hearts of men? The very angels of God in heaven cannot persuade the wretched and blundering children of earth as can one human being broken on the wheels of living. In love's service only wounded soldiers will do."

Sanders, the martyr, said, "Welcome the cross of Christ. . . . I feel no more pain in the fire than if I were on a bed of down." There was blessedness! There was consummate happiness!

Another martyr said, "The ringing of my chain hath been music in my ears; O what a comforter is a good conscience." Kissing the stake, he said, "I shall not lose my life but change it for better; instead of coals I shall have pearls."

You may not be called upon to suffer as the martyrs suffered, for this is an hour when Satan employs psychological warfare. Jesus said: "Men shall revile you . . . and shall say all manner of evil against you falsely, for my sake."[22] The tongue often inflicts a more painful wound than does the sword. To be laughed at is harder to take than to be flogged.

Some in reading this may feel that because they are not at present being persecuted, they are not living godly lives. That is not necessarily so. While there are countries where today to be an active Christian is to court death and worse, we live in a predominantly Christian country where active persecution is at a minimum.

Our environment, as well as the age in which we live, has much to do with the amount of persecution a Christian will be called upon to bear. I have known certain overly eager Christians who actually courted persecution for fear that otherwise they would not be living godly enough lives.

Remember, not all Christians are called upon to suffer at all times. Even our Lord increased in wisdom and knowledge and in favor with God and man. But the periods of popularity did not last. It ended on a cross. The important thing is to walk

[22] Matthew 5:11.

with Christ. Live for Christ! Have one consuming passion in life—to please Him! And let the chips fall where they may. As someone has said, "Never take one step out of the pathway of duty either to take a cross or to escape one."

W. C. Burns of India wrote, "Oh, to have a martyr's heart if not a martyr's crown!"

Popularity and adulation are far more dangerous for the Christian than persecution. It is easy when all goes smoothly to lose our sense of balance and our perspective. We must learn like Paul "how to abound" and "how to be abased." We must learn in "whatsoever state" we are "therewith to be content."

As we have said, the important thing is to walk with Christ, to live for Christ, and to have one consuming passion to please Him. Then, whatever happens, we know that He has permitted it in order to teach us some priceless lesson and to perfect us for His service. He will enrich our circumstances, be they pleasant or disagreeable, by the fact of His presence with us.

Three Hebrew children were cast into the burning fiery furnace, but the king said: "Lo, I see *four* men loose, walking in the midst of the fire, and they have no hurt; and the form of the fourth is like the Son of God."[22]

[22] Daniel 3:25.

X.

STEPS TO HAPPINESS

King George V wrote on the flyleaf of the Bible of a friend: "The secret of happiness is not to do what you like to do, but to learn to like what you have to do."

Too many think of happiness as some sort of will-o'-the-wisp thing that is discovered by constant and relentless searching. It is something that is not found by seeking. It is not an end in itself. Pots of gold are never found at the end of the rainbow, as we used to think when we were children; gold is mined from the ground or panned laboriously from a mountain stream.

Jesus once told his disciples: "Seek ye first the kingdom of God, and his righteousness; and all these things shall be added unto you."[1] The "things" He spoke of were the things that make men feel happy and secure: food, drink, clothes, shelter. He told us not to make these the chief goal of our lives but to "seek the kingdom," and these needs would be automatically supplied.

There, if we will take it, is the secret of happiness: "Seek ye first the kingdom of God . . . and all . . . shall be added unto you."

In the foregoing pages we have tried to interpret Jesus's formula for happiness. We realize that in many ways the interpretation falls short, both in content and clarity. The more we read this introduction to the Sermon on the Mount, the more wisdom we see hidden in it and the more convinced we are that if it is read thoughtfully and prayerfully and applied to life that a richer, fuller happiness will ensue.

In summing up the secret of happiness within the framework

[1] Matthew 6:33.

of the Beatitudes, we would like to suggest several steps to the abundant life:

Recognize your spiritual poverty.

Don't let your pride say, "I am rich, and increased with goods, and have need of nothing."[2] Remember that your own righteousness is as filthy rags and that salvation is not of works but is the gift of God. Keep ever in your mind the first Beatitude: "Blessed are the poor in spirit: for theirs is the kingdom of heaven."

God measures men by the small dimension of humility and not by the bigness of their achievements or the size of their capabilities.

Make sure you have received Christ.

Remember, it is not creeds, culture, or even respectability that saves us. It is Christ. The Bible says: "But as many as received him, to them gave he power to become the sons of God, even to them that believe on his name."[3]

Let us say that you wanted to go to Southampton, England, on the *Queen Elizabeth*. You might go to New York and get information about the *Queen Elizabeth*. You might be convinced that she is a safe, trustworthy craft and that thousands of passengers have crossed the Atlantic on her. You might even affirm your faith in her by saying, "I believe she is a good boat and that she is well able to take me to Southampton." You might do all of that and never get across the Atlantic.

To know about Christ is not enough. To be convinced that he is the Savior of the world is not enough. To affirm your faith in Him, as we do in the Apostles' Creed, is not enough. To believe that He has saved others is not enough. You really don't actively believe in Christ until you make a commitment of your life to him and receive him as your Savior.

You can best demonstrate your faith in a bank by putting your money in it. You can best show your faith in a doctor by trusting him with your physical welfare in times of illness. You can best prove your faith in a boat by getting aboard and going some place on it. You can best demonstrate your faith

[2] Revelation 3:17.

[3] John 1:12.

in Christ by trusting him with your life and receiving him un-conditionally as your Savior.

Maintain a contrite spirit.

The Bible says: "A broken and a contrite heart, O God, thou wilt not despise."[4] Let a continual flow of confession emanate from your heart. Remember it was to Christians that John wrote: "If we confess our sins, he is faithful and just to forgive us our sins, and to cleanse us from all unright-eousness."[5]

A cultured person is quick with a courteous apology when he has done wrong. If a gentleman stumbles over a lady's foot in a drawing room, he doesn't wait a week to say, "I beg your pardon!" He begs forgiveness immediately.

When you break God's law, utter a hasty, bitter word, or even think an evil thought, immediately you should confess this sin to God. And in accordance with His Word, He will forgive and cleanse your heart and transform you into His likeness.

Be sensitive to the needs of others.

In the eternal triangle of Christianity, God is first, others are second, and self is last. "Rejoice with them that do rejoice, and weep with them that weep."[6] Be sympathetic, tolerant, and understanding. Remember the third secret of happiness: "Blessed are they that mourn: for they shall be comforted."

There is no joy in life like the joy of sharing. Don't be con-tent to have too much when millions in the world have too little. Remember every time you read the Bible that millions have no Bible to read. Bear in mind when you hear the gospel preached that more than half the world has never heard the gospel story. Let your life, your means, and your prayers be shared with those millions who at this moment are wondering who will be the first to help them, Christians or Communists.

Don't be a half-Christian.

There are too many of them in the world already. The world has a profound respect for a man who is sincere in his faith.

[4] Psalm 51:17.

[5] I John 1:9.

[6] Romans 12:15.

The Bible tells us that we can't serve God and Mammon, that no man can serve two masters. Too many Christians, so called, are like the little chameleon which adapts its coloration to that of its surroundings. Even a gainsaying world is quick to recognize a real Christian and just as quick to detect a counterfeit.

Live a surrendered life.

The Bible is very explicit at this point. It says: "Know ye not, that to whom ye yield yourselves servants to obey, his servants ye are to whom ye obey; whether of sin unto death, or of obedience unto righteousness."[7]

A friend of David Livingstone's once said: "When I watched Livingstone carry out the 'leave all and follow me' life, I became a Christian in spite of myself." The world knows no greater challenge than the surrendered life.

Sherwood Eddy interviewed twenty young Communists in Moscow one day and asked each one how many hours he gave to the Party each day. Not one of them gave less than three hours in advocating the virtues of the Party, and some of them gave as many as nine hours each day, witnessing for their political beliefs. He said that it seemed Karl Marx had more witnesses in this generation than Jesus Christ. Little wonder that Christianity has not forged ahead in this generation. Surrender to God!

Be filled with the Spirit.

Men who have moved the world have been Spirit-filled. Filled with the Spirit, the first disciples "turned the world upside down." Filled with the Spirit, the reformers started the spiritual blaze which became the Reformation. Filled with the Spirit, John and Charles Wesley, working out of Oxford University, saved a great nation from moral and political collapse. Filled with the Spirit, Francis Asbury, George Fox, Jonathan Edwards, Charles Finney, and David Brainard set the mountains and prairies of America aglow with the fires of real religion. Filled with the Spirit, D. L. Moody and Ira Sankey shook two continents out of their spiritual lethargy. The tides of civilization have risen, the courses of nations have

[7] Romans 6:16.

111

been changed and the pages of history have been brightened by men who have been filled with the Spirit of God.

The Bible says to a generation much given to alcoholism and overindulgence in pleasure: "Be not drunk with wine, wherein is excess; but be filled with the Spirit."[8]

Seek to produce the fruit of the Spirit in your life.

The Bible says: "The fruit of the Spirit is love, joy, peace, long-suffering, gentleness, goodness, faith, meekness, temperance."[9]

You say, "I am powerless to produce such fruit. It would be utterly impossible for me to do so!"

With that I agree! That is, you can't produce it in your own strength. Remember, the Book says: "The fruit of the *Spirit* is love, joy, peace, long-suffering, gentleness, goodness, faith, meekness, temperance. When the Spirit of God dwells in you, *He* will produce the fruit. It is yours only to cultivate the soil of your heart through sincere devotion and yieldedness that He might find favorable ground to produce that which He will.

You might have a fruit tree in your yard; but if the soil isn't enriched and the bugs carefully destroyed, it will not yield a full crop.

As Christians, we have the Spirit of God in us. But ours is the responsibility to keep sin out of our lives so that the Spirit can produce His fruit in us.

Become grounded in the Bible.

As Christians, we have only one authority, one compass: the Word of God.

Abraham Lincoln in a letter to a friend said: "I am profitably engaged in reading the Bible. Take all of this Book upon reason that you can and the balance upon faith, and you will live and die a better man."

Great men have made it their chief book and their reliable guide. Herbert J. Taylor, formerly international president of Rotary, told me that he begins each day by reading the Sermon on the Mount aloud.

[8] Ephesians 5:18.
[9] Galatians 5:22, 23.

112

Begin the day with the Book, and as it comes to a close let the Word speak its wisdom to your soul. Let it be the firm foundation upon which your hope is built. Let it be the Staff of Life upon which your spirit is nourished. Let it be the Sword of the Spirit which cuts away the evil of your life and fashions you in His image and likeness.

Witness for Christ.

Jesus said to you: "Ye are the light of the world. . . . Let your light so shine before men, that they may see your good works, and glorify your Father which is in heaven."[10]

One faithful witness is worth a thousand mute professors of religion.

Tom Allan, Scotland's famous young preacher, was brought to Christ while a colored soldier was singing "Were You There When They Crucified My Lord?" He said it was neither the song nor the voice, but the spirit in which that soldier sang—something about his manner, something about his sincerity of expression—that convicted him of his wicked life and turned him to the Savior.

Our faith grows by expression. If we want to keep our faith, we must share it—we must witness!

Practice the Presence of God.

Jesus said: "Lo, I am with you alway, even unto the end of the world."[11] Remember, Christ is always near you. Say nothing that you would not wish to say in His presence. Do nothing that you would not do in His presence. Go to no place that you would not go in His presence. But He is not with you just to judge or condemn you; He is near to comfort, protect, guide, encourage, strengthen, cleanse and help. He will not only be with you until the "end of the world," but He will be with you "world without end." He will be with you throughout all eternity.

Learn the exercise of prayer.

Jesus said: "Men ought always to pray, and not to faint."[12]

[10] Matthew 5:14, 16.

[11] Matthew 28:20.

[12] Luke 18:1.

He said on another occasion: "Pray to thy Father which is in secret; and thy Father which seeth in secret shall reward thee openly."[13]

Prayer is not just asking. It is listening for God's orders.

Frank Laubach says: "Prayer at its highest is a two-way conversation; and for me, the most important part is listening to God's replies."

The world's great Christians have set regular hours for prayer. John Wesley arose at four in the morning and started the day with prayer, followed by an hour's Bible study.

I suggest an established time for communication with God. Make a date with Him and keep it. You'll never regret such a practice, for the "fervent prayer of a righteous man availeth much."[14]

Develop a taste for spiritual things.

"Happy are they which do hunger and thirst after righteousness: for they shall be filled."

Spiritual tastes, like physical tastes, can be cultivated. I didn't used to like yogurt, but they told me that it was good for me, so I kept trying to like it and now I'm very fond of it.

It will not be easy at first to read the Bible, witness and pray. But after you experience the strength that can come from these means of grace, they will become part of your routine, as much as breathing and eating. These are the things that give strength to the soul.

Don't be critical of others.

Habitual criticism can stifle your spiritual growth. Don't build yourself up at the expense of others. If you praise others, then others will praise you. But if you condemn others, they in turn will condemn you. Criticism begets criticism, but praise begets praise. As Jesus said: "Happy are the merciful: for they shall obtain mercy."

Don't be envious of others.

Two of the most devastating sins of today are envy and covetousness. Envying others can work havoc in your spiritual life and sap you of your spiritual strength. It also can ruin

[13] Matthew 6:6.
[14] James 5:16.

your social batting average and weaken your Christian testimony. Don't be enslaved by this ruinous evil! It can destroy your happiness and rob your life of its sweetness.

Love everybody.

The Bible says: "Let love be without dissimulation. Abhor that which is evil; cleave to that which is good."[15] This Scripture says: "*Let* love," as if it were possible for us to hinder love from being all that it should be. The love of Christ, if unhindered and unblocked by our prejudices and our malices, will embrace everyone. Christ *in* us will go on loving even the unlovely if He is not hindered by our selfishness.

Stand courageously for the right.

Horace Pitkin, the son of a wealthy merchant, was converted and went to China as a missionary. He wrote to his friends in America, saying: "It will be but a short time till we know definitely whether we can serve Him better above or here." Shortly afterward, a mob stormed the gate of the compound where Pitkin defended the women and children. He was beheaded and his head offered at the shrine of a heathen god, while his body was thrown outside in a pit with the bodies of nine Chinese Christians. Sherwood Eddy, writing about him, said: "Pitkin won more men by his death than he ever could have won by his life."

Christ needs men today who are made of martyr stuff! Dare to take a strong, uncompromising stand for Him.

Learn to relax in Christ.

I once watched a little baby learning to walk. As long as it kept its eyes on its mother it was relaxed and in perfect balance. But as soon as it looked down at its little wobbly legs, it failed.

Simon Peter found it possible to walk over the waves of Galilee as long as he kept his eyes on Christ, but when he looked away from the Savior he sank.

These are turbulent times in which we live. Men are harassed with tensions, fears, and phobias. Nothing can relieve the tensions of life like a valid faith in Christ.

Personally, in my crusade work when called upon to speak

15 Romans 12:9.

often two or three times to crowds of many thousands, I find myself growing nervous and tense. When these tensions begin mounting, I find a place to lie down in complete relaxation. After a quiet, simple prayer, I repeat the words in simple faith: "I can do all things through Christ which strengtheneth me." It is then that I become fully conscious of His strength-giving Presence. On occasions, I have come out of stadium meetings, having spoken to huge audiences under most unfavorable conditions, as fresh and invigorated as though I had just had a full night's sleep.

You, too, can learn to relax in Christ!

Don't be a victim of paranoia.

In other words, don't be hypersensitive to criticism or entertain an exaggerated sense of your own importance. This is the secret of unhappiness. Many egocentric people are victims of this terrible disease of the mind. If people never actually criticize them, they at least imagine that they do, and they suffer the agonies of a mental inferno.

The paranoid sees two acquaintances talking together somewhat seriously, and immediately he imagines that they are discussing his faults. He retreats into the torture chamber of his own evil mind where he manufactures misery in wholesale lots. Run from paranoia as you would run from a plague.

Remember you are immortal and will live forever.

To expect absolute, unqualified bliss in this life is expecting a bit too much. Remember, this life is only the dressing room for eternity. In the Beatitudes Jesus said that in this life there are persecution, slander, libel and deception. But He also said: "Rejoice, and be exceeding glad: for great is your reward in heaven."[16]

He strongly hinted that relative happiness in this life is related to an absolute happiness in the after life. Here we have an "earnest" of our inheritance, but in heaven we come into our full estate of happiness.

The Christian thinks and acts within the framework of eternity. He is not embittered when things don't turn out the way he planned. He knows that the sufferings of this

16 Matthew 5:12.

present world are not worthy to be compared with the glory that shall be revealed hereafter. So he rejoices and is exceedingly glad!

In the covered wagon days when the Old West was bulging with gold, the pioneers endured the sufferings of the prairies, the mountains, and the desert, and the savage attacks of the Indians because they knew that beyond those Sierras lay the rewards of golden California.

When Bill Borden, son of the wealthy Bordens, went out to China as a missionary, many of his friends thought he was foolish to "waste his life," as they put it, trying to convert a few heathens to Christianity. But Bill loved Christ and he loved men! He hadn't been out there very long before he contracted an oriental disease and died. At his bedside they found a note that he had written while he was dying. It read: "No reserve, no retreat, and no regrets."

Bill had found more happiness in his few years of sacrificial service than most people find in a lifetime.

Many thousands of rational, cultured citizens of the earth have found happiness in Christ. You can too! But, remember, you will never find it by searching directly for it. As the Lord of happiness said: "Seek ye first the kingdom of God, and His righteousness; and all these things shall be added unto you."[17]

[17] Matthew 6:33.

23761